Gather the GOODNESS

A WORD*Girls* Collective

A WORD*Girls* Collective

Foreword by WordGirls Founder, Kathy Carlton Willis

Gather the
GOODNESS

A Taste of Kindness, Gentleness & More

3G Books

Gather the Goodness ©2025 by Kathy Carlton Willis
www.kathycarltonwillis.com
ISBN 979-8-9888761-2-0
Published by 3G Books, Tyler, TX 75703

All rights reserved. No part of this book may be reproduced, stored in a retrieval system, or transmitted in any form or by any means—electronic, mechanical, photocopy, recording, or otherwise—without written permission of the publisher, except for brief quotations in printed reviews.

To protect individual privacy, some names and identifying details have been altered.

Scripture quotations marked NLT are taken from the *Holy Bible*, New Living Translation, copyright © 1996, 2004, 2015 by Tyndale House Foundation. Used by permission of Tyndale House Publishers, Inc., Carol Stream, Illinois 60188. All rights reserved.

Scripture quotations marked ESV are from The Holy Bible, English Standard Version. ESV® Text Edition: 2016. Copyright © 2001 by Crossway Bibles, a publishing ministry of Good News Publishers.

Scripture quotations marked AMP are taken from the Amplified® Bible, Copyright © 2015 by The Lockman Foundation. La Habra, CA 90631. All rights reserved. Used by permission. www.lockman.org

Scripture quotations marked MSG are taken from *THE MESSAGE*, copyright © 1993, 2002, 2018 by Eugene H. Peterson. Used by permission of NavPress. All rights reserved. Represented by Tyndale House Publishers, Inc.

Scriptures marked NKJV are taken from the New King James Version®. Copyright © 1982 by Thomas Nelson. Used by permission. All rights reserved.

The original version of "The Winding Trail" by Sally Ferguson first appeared at vinewords.net.

Copyedited by Kathy Carlton Willis

Editing, Interior, and Cover Design by Michelle Rayburn
www.missionandmedia.com

Contents

Foreword ix

About WordGirls. xv

KINDNESS

From Bedraggled to Blessed *Barb Syvertson*
Essay 3

The Queen of Third Grade *Lisa-Anne Wooldridge*
Devotion 9

Seeds of Kindness *Sandy Lipsky*
Essay 13

Lightening the Load *Beth Kirkpatrick*
Devotion 19

A Serving of Kindness *Robin Steinweg*
Short Story. 23

Getting the Runaround *Charlaine Martin*
Short Story. 29

Glimmers on the Water *Lisa-Anne Wooldridge*
Essay 35

Sharing the Unbearable *Joni Topper*
Essay 41

Kindling Kindness *Carolyn Gaston*
Essay 47

A Little Kindness Goes Far *Diana Leagh Matthews*
Devotion 53

GOODNESS

When Goodness Passes By *Kolleen Lucariello*
Essay 59

Goodness and Merci *Lisa-Anne Wooldridge*
Fiction 65

Marvelous Mosaics *Carolyn Gaston*
Poetry 69

The Lost Bike *Victoria Hanan Romo*
Devotion 73

The Winding Trail *Sally Ferguson*
Devotion 79

Remember God's Goodness *Dawn Marie Wilson*
Devotion 83

I Know God Is Good *Carolyn Gaston*
Poetry 89

Goodness Rocks *Pattie Reitz*
Essay 91

Savoring God's Goodness *Charlaine Martin*
Devotion 97

Lift from Below *Robin Steinweg*
Essay 101

How Do You Hide a Mountain? *Janice Metot*
Essay 105

Good Gracious *Kathy Carlton Willis*
Poetry 111

When Goodness Takes the Helm *Joni Topper*
Bible Study 113

FAITHFULNESS

He Rescues Me *Denise Margaret Ackerman*
Poetry 121

RV There, God? *Kolleen Lucariello*
Essay 123

Faith in Sioux Falls *Hally J. Wells*
Essay 127

Wellspring for Weariness *Becki James*
Devotion 133

Fresh Each Day *Denise Margaret Ackerman*
Devotion 137

God Cares for the Lost *Denise Margaret Ackerman*
Bible Study 141

Let It Flow, Sistahs! *Mindy Cantrell*
Bible Study 151

Surrender *Joni Topper*
Poetry 157

Safe with My Father *Joni Topper*
Essay 159

The Land of Rainbows *Lisa-Anne Wooldridge*
Essay 163

When the Mountain Won't Move *Betty Predmore*
Essay 169

A Tapestry of Faithfulness *Joanie Shawhan*
Poetry 173

GENTLENESS

Robot Vacs and Human Hearts *Hally J. Wells*
Devotion 179

Stained-Glass Love *Lisa-Anne Wooldridge*
Poetry 183

Gentleness on Display *Joni Topper*
Devotion 185

Gentleness Is Power *Sandy Lipsky*
Devotion 189

Gentle Words *Julia Thompson*
Fiction 193

Leaning into God's Gentleness *Becki James*
Devotion 199

That's Bananas! *Lisa-Anne Wooldridge*
Devotion 203

In Gentleness He Stooped *Joanie Shawhan*
Poetry 207

The Enemy of Gentleness *Denise Margaret Ackerman*
Devotion 209

Wardrobe Malfunctions *Kathy Carlton Willis*
Bible Study 213

Takes a Big Dog to Weigh a Ton *Beth Kirkpatrick*
Devotion 219

Our Contributors 223

Acknowledgments 233

WordGirls Collective Books 235

A Foreword by Our Founder

Remember all those home decor signs with the word *gather*? I found it sad and sort of funny that right after I had a friend hand paint a gather sign for me, the pandemic hit, and no one was gathering anymore. My two small groups disbanded, and we ended up moving to a strange town where we knew no one. Whenever my eyes settle on that sign, there's this tremendous longing to gather. Missing it made me miss it, ya know?

But there are other ways we gather. Not just physically in the community of groups. This book helps us focus on *gather* in a new way. We're gathering the goodness and all her friends. Friends like kindness, faithfulness, and gentleness—virtues mentioned in the list of the fruit of the Spirit. *Gather the Goodness* helps us explore God displaying these attributes and also how the Spirit expresses these qualities through believers.

What is the source of the fruit of the Spirit? The obvious answer is not a *what* but a *who*. The Holy Spirit, of course. But let's look deeper. If we didn't have love, we wouldn't have gentleness, goodness, kindness, or faithfulness. Love is the root. Not fear. Not obligation. Not works.

GATHER THE GOODNESS

- Where there is love, *kindness* reaches out to someone despite what others might think.

- Where there is love, *goodness* notices the needs of someone who feels invisible.

- Where there is love, *faithfulness* stays loyal no matter the cost.

- Where there is love, *gentleness* helps us want to care for someone who is hurting.

Often, we're more likely to hope for (or even expect) these virtues from others as they show us love than we are to consistently live it out in our own lives. One of the intents for the book is to realize, sort of like the Wizard of Oz and Dorothy, that what we long for from God and others are the very things we need to develop more in ourselves. And it's been in us all along. Not red slippers, but Holy Spirit. When we open ourselves up to his work through us, these others-focused attributes can become our mission and purpose.

I'm so glad God's Spirit grows these in and through us rather than depending on my works to get them accomplished. This maturing process happens as we spend time with God—but how can we do that? By focusing on his presence in our lives. Listening to his words that come like nudges of wisdom and love. Reading the Bible (that's one way he talks to us). Talking to him in prayer. We know we've been with God when we experience peace that makes no human sense.

Let's look at the Spirit's fruit at work.

Kindness Notices

Think about the times you've needed kindness. The only way someone could be kind to you was if they noticed your need. This reminds me of Jesus's compassion. "When he saw the crowds, he had compassion on them because they were confused and helpless, like sheep without a shepherd."[1]

A great way to be a part of God's work is to pay attention to those who need compassion. The hard part is we'll have to go out of our way to do this—outside of a focus on our own needs and our own schedules. Often, the opportunities to notice where kindness is needed will happen at inconvenient times or with people outside of our comfort zone.

Some of the times I've experienced the loving act of kindness are when God placed it on someone's heart to reach out to me. It overwhelms me with the knowledge that not only do they care, but that God cares, to nudge them to be kind to me. It's one way I know God is in my life. When we've experienced such love, we want to share it. Let's make it a matter of prayer for God to help us notice where kindness is needed.

Goodness Nourishes

What does it mean to nourish someone? It can mean the simple act of feeding them nourishment. But it can also mean to encourage and nurture them.[2] We've all experienced undeserved goodness in our lives, and we've also seen it displayed in someone. That's right, goodness is both an internal quality and an external result. We can't have the outward works of goodness without it starting in our hearts as a pure and holy trait.

God nourishes us, and that is how goodness grows in our souls. And because of that growth cycle, God equips us with the resources to be truly good to others, with no expectation of perfect performance or anything in return.

---

1. Matthew 9:36 (NLT)
2. *Merriam-Webster.com Dictionary*, s.v. "nourish," accessed March 31, 2025, https://www.merriam-webster.com/dictionary/nourish.

The motive for goodness is always love, not to be told we've done well. In fact, with goodness, we're not even focused on self but on God at work in the lives of others. I can't help but imagine a seed planted and the death and growth cycle it goes through to feed someone.

Faithfulness Navigates

Let's think through all the ways faithfulness functions in God's kingdom. He is faithful to us. We are faithful to him. Others are faithful to us. We are faithful to them. Faithfulness at its best is a four-way expression of love that helps navigate relationships.

One of the acts that will kill a relationship more than any other is being unfaithful. This isn't only reserved for married couples. I've seen hearts broken by friends who stabbed them in the back (is that a medical side effect of said stabbing?). People loyal to their job or their church or their family yet didn't receive loyalty in return.

Faithfulness is more than loyalty, though. It's also being full of faith. Faith in the one we place our trust in. We can be faithful because God is truth, and the truth sets us free. Faithfulness is consistent, which makes it reliable. Faithfulness obeys God rather than wavering in doubt.

When we offer faithfulness to others, they get to experience the gift of love in a way that they really long for. Someone who is dependable and trustworthy.

Gentleness Nurtures

Each member of the Trinity expresses gentleness in different ways. With all the triggers in our lives, it's consoling to think of the *gentle Trinity*.

God the Father has so much patience with us. He nurtures us with tender-loving care. His forgiveness gently welcomes us into his fold.

When God the Son interacts with people, his gentleness is evident. He distributed care equally, no matter their religion, their sinfulness, or their reputation. He specializes in broken people. His ministry on earth was all about restoration and healing as he served others.

God the Holy Spirit portrays gentleness in the way he comforts and guides us. He even shines the light on our sin gently, giving us the control to turn from our sin or to remain in it. It's obvious that gentleness is a central feature of God's being.

When we are gentle as God is gentle, we live a life of compassion, patience, tender reconciliation, and humility. We invite others into the rest we can have in God (and that means we need to enter into that rest ourselves!).

Gather the Goodness

What are you gathering these days? I can attest that some of my possessions are gathering dust, and my body sometimes gathers a few extra pounds. But what I cherish most is gathering goodness, along with her friends: kindness, faithfulness, and gentleness. This WordGirls collective is a true anthology. A gathering of devotions, fictional short stories, poetry, mini-Bible studies, essays, and more. Our prayer is that you will discover words that lighten your load and draw you closer to the *gentle Trinity.*

Because of love,

Kathy Carlton Willis, WordGirls Founder and God's Grin Gal

About WordGirls

Eleven years ago (2014), I had a brainchild to start a group to coach fun, faith-filled women who were serious about the writing life. I served on faculty at national writer's conferences and realized attendees remained stuck in the writing process. They were often overwhelmed by the conference material and didn't know how to apply it to their writing lives. I'd see them return year after year with their projects showing little progress. They needed a group to keep them accountable and a coach to help them figure out their next steps.

WordGirls is a special sisterhood of writing support for women who write from a biblical worldview (whether for the faith market or general market). We propel writers to the next level—regardless of where they are today.

Here's an overview of our exclusive WordGirls benefits:

1. Once-per-year individual phone coaching to personalize your advancement as a writer and/or speaker.

2. Private Facebook group to interact, brainstorm, pray for each other, share ideas, ask questions, etc.

3. Monthly topics to help you grow as a writer. To enhance your learning, we will cover the topics through Facebook group discussions and Zoom live sessions (recorded for you to watch later if you can't make it live).

4. The Blessing Seat think tanks during our video meetings (more details below).

5. Downloadable PDFs offer extra training in the form of tutorials.

6. Weekly study hall. We designate Fridays to work on projects we call our B.I.C. time (butt in chair). Study hall provides added accountability. (If you can't make it, we cheer you on whenever you designate your B.I.C. time.)

7. Periodic challenges. Some challenges are month-long, and others last a season. These challenges will stretch you without overwhelming you. They are guaranteed to increase productivity if you participate. (Participation is not required to be a member.)

8. Digital membership badge to post on your website or social media page.

9. Reduced rates for events and for-fee materials. We have online retreats and WordGirls@Home intensives. We offer WordGirls Getaways as circumstances allow.

10. Opportunity to submit writing for our WordGirls publications.

11. Additional services when you hire our coach for a reduced hourly rate only available to members.

Around-the-Clock B.I.C. Relay

We host two twenty-four-hour B.I.C. relays a year. Members commit to writing for at least one hour. Some do more, and some time slots have two members, but added together, we work around the clock. We imagine we are on a relay race, passing the baton to the writer taking over the next time slot. As we pass the baton, we pray for them. Many participants use the team roster as a prayer list and pray for everyone by name. We send prayer notes and posts to each other to encourage and cheer on. It is quite uplifting! Members say their productivity levels surge during our special relays—thanks to the extra inspiration and motivation.

Books

In 2020, WordGirls created a group-funded compilation book that released in March 2021: *Wit, Whimsy & Wisdom*. Our second book released in November 2021: *Snapshots of Hope & Heart*. While the first two books are devotionals, our third and fourth books are collections of essays. *Live & Learn: Unexpected Lessons from God's Classroom* released in 2022, and we had a fun and meaningful virtual book club with readers going through the book together. In 2023, we published *Sage, Salt & Sunshine: Women Inspiring Women with Insight, Truth, Light & Joy*. With two cups on the cover, it's the perfect inspiration for a women's tea or book club group. It celebrates the positive influence other women have as they pour into us. Now, it's our turn to pour into others. The devotional *Love, Joy & Peace* released in 2024. We hosted a virtual road trip to celebrate this fun theme.

    Who may submit to WordGirls writing projects? Anyone who is a member at some time during the same calendar year as the call for submissions or attended a WordGirls intensive, getaway, or retreat during that year.

The Blessing Seat

Some mastermind groups have an interactive process called the hot seat. A member shares their project with the group and receives input and brainstorming, much like a think tank. We decided the term "hot seat" made it sound like a high-pressure inquisition! So, our group offers a grace-filled version of a think tank called The Blessing Seat. We assist members in getting their questions answered and their projects propelled to the next stage.

Size of Group

To keep the group intimate, we grant a limited number of memberships. We only have open enrollment twice per year: in January (for a February to January membership period) and in July (for an August to July membership period). You'll find a registration form at kathycarltonwillis.com/wordgirls. If you have questions, email kathy@kathycarltonwillis.com.

We also open up the online and in-person retreats to non-members, so keep an eye on the website for details of upcoming events.

Kindness

From Bedraggled to Blessed

by Barb Syvertson

"**WAS THE BABY** crying when you left home?" my coworker asked as I walked into the office that night.

"Yes! How did you know?"

"Because you have drool and slobber all down your shoulder and in your hair. I figured it wasn't yours."

Bedraggled Mom

It had been a tough day. All three kids were sick, and I hated to leave my husband with chaos that night. Our baby wasn't happy that I was leaving. I wasn't thrilled either. Working this evening shift was not my dream job, but it added some money to our tight budget and paid for luxuries like fresh fruit and dental work. I hoped to get my quota done quickly so I could leave early.

At the completion of my work, my supervisor discovered a careless but critical error I had made. She was not happy, and neither was I. We stayed an hour longer than our usual shift to fix the error and redo the work. My short ten-minute dinner break didn't happen.

This created a perfect environment for a pity party—with no guests invited. Once I was in the privacy of my car, I released a week's worth of built-up tears. I cried because I was exhausted and hungry. I cried because of my reprimand. I cried because my kiddos were sick, and we were poor. Ultimately, I felt big-time sorry for myself. I didn't pray. I didn't sing praise songs. I didn't phone a friend. I just cried and drove too fast.

I didn't pray. I didn't sing praise songs. I didn't phone a friend. I just cried and drove too fast.

Benevolent Officer

When I noticed the police siren and flashing lights behind me, I knew I was getting an expensive ticket. I felt such shame. As the policeman approached my car, I'm sure he heard me sobbing. He could probably tell my crying had started long before he pulled me over.

"Are you okay, ma'am?"

In between sobs, I revealed, "I got in trouble at work, my kids are sick, we have no money. I'm working nights to make ends meet, and now they won't."

His soft response was, "I'm so sorry. I'm not going to give you a ticket tonight, but I need you to slow down. I'm worried about you. I'll follow you home to make sure you get there safely." He spoke like a compassionate father.

He quietly drove behind me and waited in his patrol car until I got into the house. I never noticed the name on his badge, but I definitely noticed his kindness. It was something I didn't think I deserved. He noticed me, not as the driver of a speeding van at midnight but as a young mom who was a hot mess.

This incident serves as a reminder that God loves me. That he doesn't treat me as my actions deserve. That he can and does prompt people to make his kindness shine in the dark hours of a random Tuesday night. That he loves me despite an absent-minded error. He loves me when I ugly cry and even when I speed. God's kindness is like that. It notices, soothes, heals, and cares. It whispers a word of hope to us if we listen.

Bereaved Mother-in-Law

My lessons in God's kindness have continued over the years. Last year, I did something I'd never done before. I read the book of Ruth (in the Bible) daily for the whole month of May. It was fairly short. It's in story form, and I love stories. What I didn't expect to learn was that this Old Testament account is drenched in kindness. The story picks up when the main characters experience a time of deep turmoil and grief.

Naomi becomes a widow, and ten years after moving to the foreign land of Moab, her two sons die. She decides to return to her roots in Bethlehem, where she hopes to survive better around familiarity. Naomi tells her widowed daughters-in-law, Orpah and Ruth, to go back to their original homes and asks the Lord to show them kindness because they had been so kind to their husbands and to her. She further encourages them to go back by admitting that her life is too bitter for them to be around her. Orpah concedes and returns to her family, but Ruth lovingly relocates with Naomi.

They show up in Bethlehem tired, sad, and poor. Filled with bitterness, Naomi has a pity party of her own. She complains that although years ago she left Bethlehem very full, now God was bringing her back empty. Her depression and self-pity distort the fact that when she and her husband left Bethlehem it had been because of a famine. However, when she returns it is harvesting time. Naomi doesn't own farmable land, but Ruth offers to gather fallen grain in a nearby field. If

I were Ruth, my motivation might have been to get away from a bitter mother-in-law, but thankfully, Ruth's motivation is love.

Benevolent Landowner

Ruth ends up in a field belonging to Boaz. The Bible describes him as a prominent man of noble character.[3] His thoughtful generosity changes Ruth and Naomi's circumstances. Ruth arrives home with so much food that it is almost too heavy to carry. Boaz is protective of her from the day they meet, and he continues to ensure she is treated with respect. He is a relative of her husband, which had significant benefits for a widow in those days.

It's a beautiful story where gentleness, goodness, faithfulness, and kindness are displayed in great measure.

It's a beautiful story where gentleness, goodness, faithfulness, and kindness are displayed in great measure. Boaz and Ruth get married and give birth to their son, Obed, who becomes David's grandfather. And in Matthew chapter one, there is a list of thirty generations from Boaz and Ruth to the birth of Jesus. Very few women are named in this impressive list of ancestors, but Ruth's name is there along with Boaz's.

Beloved Reminder

Thirty years after my pity party, I still remember that night so clearly. Was it the most devastating time of my life? No! But it was a time when God showed his love for me through the timely kindness of a stranger. Some acts of kindness improve your day, like the tenderness of the

---

3. Ruth 2:1

police officer that dark night. And as in the case of Ruth and Boaz, some acts of kindness impact history.

The day Ruth showed up in Boaz's field began as any other day for him. Gentleness was already a part of his daily pattern. Boaz had no idea that history books would someday tell his story. He had no idea that the Savior of the world would be his descendant. I am thankful for both of these stories because they remind me that small kindnesses are seeds God uses to proclaim his love. When you show kindness to others, you have no idea what impact it may have on people's lives outside of your reach and beyond your earthly life.

We prove ourselves by our purity, our understanding, our patience, our kindness, by the Holy Spirit within us, and by our sincere love.

2 Corinthians 6:6 (nlt)

The Queen of Third Grade

by Lisa-Anne Wooldridge

Kind words are like honey—sweet to the soul and healthy for the body.

PROVERBS 16:24 (NLT)

I WAS A BIT of a misfit as a child. In those days, I was too skinny, had Coke-bottle glasses, and wore all the wrong clothes. It didn't help that I was reading years ahead of my grade level and raised my hand to answer questions far too often. I was not part of the "in-crowd," and yes, there's an in-crowd even in the third grade. One thing I did have was a wonderful relationship with Jesus, aided by a Sunday school teacher who was big on loving your neighbor.

One afternoon, a little girl in my class did something surprising. We were both eight-year-olds, but she was everything I wasn't. She was the prettiest girl in school. Her family was well-off, and she was well-liked by everyone. Her popularity could be measured by the multiple birthday party invitations she received every week, even from kids in other grades. On this day, she asked the teacher if she could rearrange the tables and assign where everyone sat. The teacher, who favored her, said yes.

Everyone snickered as she started gathering up the misfits in class, asking them to move to a certain table and the kids already there to trade seats with them. I was already at that table, and she left me there. You could feel the change in the air; it seemed like we were being grouped together because we didn't fit in. The teacher looked a bit concerned, but she let it play out. Then the popular girl did something I never expected. She sat down. Right there at the head of the misfit table, she sat down and smiled at all of us. Even at that young age, I knew I'd just witnessed some sort of holy, defiant act. She'd made herself one of us.

There are no misfits in the presence of love.

We would have crowned her our queen, but we didn't get the chance. The first thing she did was tell each one of us why she wanted to sit at a table with us. First up, a little boy named James who was often picked on. She said he was the nicest boy in the school because he never did the same mean things back that other people did to him. She turned to me and said she'd always wanted a smart friend who was as kind as I was. She told another girl, who was very chaotic, how creative she was and that she always picked beautiful, fun things to wear. This little girl started the trend of mismatched everything—I'm sure of it! Our queen's words had a deep impact on all of us at the table, and on everyone else watching and listening.

Her name is lost to me now, but the memory of her honey blonde hair, sweet smile, and her incredible act of kindness remains clear. I made up my mind—if given the chance, I'd do the same for others. She showed me God's heart. Later in life, it occurred to me that I didn't have to be in the in-crowd to love people and include them, or to tell them how wonderful they are. Because of her kindness, I learned there are no misfits in the presence of love.

> *Father, help me gather the precious ones who don't always feel they belong and give them a place of honor at the table. Show me who they are and how wonderfully you made them. Let me see everyone with your kind eyes.*

Seeds of Kindness

by Sandy Lipsky

I COULD NOT CATCH my breath. The pain took control of every sense—dulling sight, sound, taste, and smell. But my sense of touch felt heightened by a million. A visiting coach stood over me as I lay supine on a red rubber mat that rested over four automobile tires.

"Get up," he shouted.

I tried to sit, but the searing physical sensation in my arm pulled me back onto the mat. "I can't." My voice sounded weak and far away.

He grabbed my right arm to lift me out of the high jump pit.

The scream that burst from my mouth surprised us both. Immediately my left hand grasped my right elbow as if to protect it from another assault.

He rolled his eyes as he called over the coach from my school.

Both coaches soon realized I was not simply bemoaning the fact I missed the lowest height of the high jump bar at the first middle school track meet of the season.

Undeserved Kindness

The daughter of my coach volunteered to help me to the locker room. She supported my arm and spoke gently with reassuring words. Her kindness surprised me. I knew this girl. She was two years younger than me–the sister of a neighbor who lived near my best friend. Somehow, I never paid attention to her until today.

Her kindness surprised me.

My coach phoned Mom at home. We lived a block from the school. She and my sister came to whisk me off to our local doctor, who took X-rays and then sent me to an orthopedic surgeon in a nearby town.

A dark, rickety elevator shook us up to the third floor, where the specialist's office resided. The condition of this elevator did not help my anxiety. Two years prior to this event, my best friend and I were stuck in a department store elevator. When smoke began to fill the enclosed space, one of us pushed the emergency button. Within minutes, the fire department had arrived. To this day, I prefer the stairs.

After the surgeon looked at the X-rays we brought from the physician's office, he said words that took a moment to register. "You'll need surgery tomorrow. Your arm is fractured and needs pins inserted for it to heal properly."

My stomach felt like a beehive on the rampage. I glanced at the door. Flight was my first instinct, and panic provided unusual courage. "Why don't we take a day to think about it," I suggested. The bold plea fell on ears too wise to listen. I resigned myself to the doctor's decision and followed my mom to the car like a lamb to the slaughter.

The hospital smelled like my science classroom on the day we dissected rats. Bright lights highlighted the dirty stains on my white track shirt that a staff member said would need to be cut off. Dad had left work early and joined Mom, my sister, and me at the nurse's station. Hurried staff asked a myriad of questions and then led me and my family to a semi-private hospital room. The nursing assistant rushed to close the curtain to offer privacy to the other patient, but not before we saw each other. A gray-haired woman with a round, wrinkled face and a welcoming smile looked in my direction. Because visiting hours were over, my family made sure I was settled in bed and then left to go home for the night.

Unexpected Kindness

Tears flowed down my cheeks, and an uncontrollable sob broke free from my pursed lips about a minute after my family departed. I had never been in a hospital before. Alone, scared, and in terrible pain, I sucked in my lower lip and squeezed my eyes shut. This was going to be a long night. Just as fear began to burrow into my brain, I heard a gentle voice from behind the curtain.

"What's your name?"

For the next hour, my roommate and I bantered about where we were from and what brought us to the hospital. She shared about her fall on the ice in the parking lot of a local grocery store. Her broken hip had taken weeks to mend, but in the next two days, she hoped to go home.

Looking down at my puffy hand sticking out of a makeshift cast, I told her I would miss my choir concert the following evening. It was the first time I had been asked to play the piano accompaniment for a song. She listened to my stuttering, sniffling words as I talked about the performance. Her kind comments soothed my internal and external pain. This stranger I had known for an hour served as counselor, friend, and grandma and even helped me navigate the unfamiliar hospital world.

Transformed Kindness

The surgeon repaired my arm the following day. When I returned to the room, my surrogate grandma was gone. How I would miss her. The kindness she offered had given me courage and strength.

Later in the afternoon, a nurse from another floor stopped in for a visit. She introduced herself as a sister of one of my classmates. In her hand, she held a large, colorful greeting card. As she handed it to me, she said, "When Kira heard about your accident, she asked if I could bring this card to you." I smiled as I read the words on the front—*It's No Fun Being in the Hospital.* The chosen card captured my thoughts perfectly. I lifted the multi-folded gift, and a warm sensation came over me as if the sun burst forth from behind the clouds. Inside contained signatures and notes from fellow students, teachers, and friends.

At school, I hardly spoke to Kira. I mocked her for the Jesus stickers found on her folders and notebooks. If asked which friend would bring something to me in the hospital, her name wouldn't have been on my list. Despite my meanness, she reached out in kindness. Her actions surprised me. It awakened something in my heart. She had sown a seed, and I began to feel it germinate.

Like seeds, kindness often arrives in a small package.

I still have the card received decades ago. It's stapled to a page in a scrapbook along with other priceless memories. Recently as I flipped through the pages of this scrapbook, my eyes fell upon the multicolored treasure. The warmth I experienced in the hospital flooded my heart as I reflected on her selfless, loving action.

Like seeds, kindness often arrives in a small package. Such generosity may not be noticed at first, but once planted in ready soil, it takes root. When watered and nurtured, kindness has the potential for abundant growth and proliferation. Those who practice kindness rarely see the effects of their planting. I'm confident those who treated me kindly in this narrative remain unaware of their impact. Their seeds of kindness grew over time and transformed my life. I am determined to plant it forward.

So we praise God for the glorious grace he has poured out on us who belong to his dear Son. He is so rich in kindness and grace that he purchased our freedom with the blood of his Son and forgave our sins. He has showered his kindness on us, along with all wisdom and understanding.

Ephesians 1:6–8 (nlt)

Lightening the Load

by Beth Kirkpatrick

Bear one another's burdens, and so fulfill the law of Christ.

GALATIANS 6:2 (NKJV)

OH, NO! YOUR friend received bad news, and her heart is heavy. You lifted her up in prayer—now, what can you do? What would God want you to do? Anything? Nothing?

This verse from Galatians is a beautiful reminder of Jesus's words about the most important commandment. In Matthew 22, Jesus is asked which is the greatest commandment. He replies that loving God with all your heart, soul, and mind is the greatest, and combined with loving your neighbor as yourself, these form the framework of all law. Bearing our neighbor's burdens is a special level of fulfillment of God's loving law. What a beautiful way to show kindness!

But this passage is as notable for what it doesn't say as what it does. Notice that it doesn't say to give advice and solve one another's problems. Though it's natural to want to help by fixing things, it's more helpful to be present and offer a listening ear, reassuring our friend that they are being seen and heard. As listeners, we offer confidentiality and a safe place for expressing thoughts and feelings, keeping our opinions and advice to ourselves unless asked. Allowing them to speak freely can be a welcome relief to someone who is heavily burdened.

Bearing our neighbor's burdens is a special level of fulfillment of God's loving law. What a beautiful way to show kindness!

In fact, it isn't necessary to provide any counsel to minister to someone carrying a heavy burden. In the second chapter of Job, we read about his friends coming to sit with him after he had lost his family and possessions. They sat in silence for a week as they practiced the custom of shiva because they recognized the depth of his grief. Just being present with people lets them know they are not alone—we share God's peace. So often, we worry about saying the right thing when no words are needed.

One important thing this passage does say is that we are to bear *one another's* burdens. Many times, we quickly volunteer to help others but are reluctant to ask for or receive help ourselves. It's hard to admit what we might consider a weakness. But if we refuse to show vulnerability, we hide behind a mask of pretended perfection. When we don't allow others to bear our burdens, we can't grow closer to our Christian brothers and sisters. Not only that, we deprive them of the opportunity to carry our burdens and fulfill the law of Christ.

Ultimately, everyone's burdens are borne by our Savior. Scripture reminds us to cast all our cares on him because he cares for us.[4] It is

---

4. 1 Peter 5:7

amazing to realize that the Creator of the universe wants us to entrust all our worries to him—yet he does! As we share the difficulties of this world with each other, we can be encouraged that God walks beside us, sharing the load. And one day, God will lift all our burdens, and we will rejoice in an eternity of his love.

As we travel on this journey through life, help me to see those who need help carrying their burdens. Help me to listen and be a comfort to others with the peaceful presence of kindness that only you provide. May I be humble enough to ask for the help I need. And at the end of our journey, may all your people walk into the light of your eternal love, unburdened and free.

A Serving of Kindness

by Robin Steinweg

HANNAH MOVED QUICKLY and efficiently to fill the water glasses for the table of women. "Hello, ladies. How are you today? It's a cold one!"

Before they could answer, she was at the next table.

They'd had Hannah a few times now but hadn't seen their waitress Meg for a few months, the one who'd almost always served them in the past. Meg had moved on, but none of them knew where. Hannah was certainly a good server. But they'd gotten to know Meg over the years. They missed her. Before they'd gone inside that day, Shari remarked, smiling, "Meg always left us a whole handful of those wrapped mints. Nobody else goes overboard like that."

Hannah's lips stretched into an automatic smile as she zipped by to drop off a carafe of ice water. Jo thought there seemed to be a strained look about the young woman. Troubled, her eyes followed Hannah until the table conversation drew her back in.

The friends cherished time together. Their conversation covered their lives and interests all the way from national or local events to family and church-family joys and concerns. Often, they brainstormed writing, work, or ideas for volunteering. Occasionally, their talk veered to health—which, they acknowledged ruefully, seemed to be a sign of their years.

It was Shari and her intentional thoughtfulness that had first brought the women together. When her children reached their teens, she looked ahead to an empty nest. And what then? What would she do when life became narrower? When it no longer centered on her daughters' immediate care? Of course, she and her husband would always be there for the girls and each other. But Shari told Jo she couldn't imagine waiting in case of a hoped-for call.

Surely if friends linked arms and passed milestones together, they would come through it better.

Her friends would soon face the same situation, ending lifelong careers or wandering around an empty house. Shari had pondered solutions and reached out to Jo and the others. Surely if friends linked arms and passed these milestones together, she said, they would come through it better and have something to look forward to.

So, Shari started their book club. Wisdom had told her it would be best to meet with some kind of purpose, as she explained to the ladies. That way, they'd never lack for fresh topics of conversation. Books would encourage them to look outward as well as inward and keep them growing.

Inspired by Shari's idea and at the cusp of diving into an interest she hadn't seriously pursued while raising her children, Jo looked into starting a writer's group. A workshop given at the writer's conference she'd attended convinced her of the practicality of such a move. She reasoned that the two groups were sort of related, and you sure couldn't have too much of a good thing like getting together with friends! A writer's group would be a great justification for meeting a second time in the month.

Shari's initial reluctance to commit to writing was overcome by Jo's enthusiasm. They might not have anything other than personal letters to write at first, but as they learned more about the craft of writing and the publishing industry, that could change.

And it did. Each month, they and other friends from Shari's book club prepared a piece of writing to submit for positive critique. They learned of writing opportunities and began to submit work, have it accepted, and then published.

A dozen years later, the women still met monthly over a chosen book. Then, two weeks later, they'd meet to go over their writing pieces and congratulate each other on newly published work. They usually enjoyed lunch at a local restaurant afterward.

Jo was the impulsive member. At this lunch, as was usual, her attention often flitted from their conversation to a song from the overhead speakers to what was on her plate to something outside the window. The others smiled and gently "brought her back," never criticizing.

The next time Hannah paused to ask if everything was all right with their meals, Jo decided to speak. Her stomach tightened over the potential of causing embarrassment to either Hannah, her friends, or herself, but she felt compelled.

"How are you holding up? Is there anything we might pray about for you?"

Hannah only hesitated for an instant. "Actually, yes, there is." She related a scare she'd had about a heart issue, rolling back her cuff to show them the wristband recommended by her doctor to monitor her pulse. She added with an ironic tone of voice that the doctor had prescribed rest. When the friends made sounds of sympathy, she said

GATHER THE GOODNESS

the manager had scheduled her that day for two shifts. "Two!" she said. "One after the other. By the time I finish here this afternoon, I might have an hour at home before I have to be back here for the evening shift. And when am I supposed to be a mother and wife, cook dinner, take care of my family—and get rest?"

Jo spoke. "We'll pray for you." Then she added, in case Hannah thought she meant to interrupt her work and also aware of causing her friends discomfort in that public place, "We'll be praying for you."

"Thank you, I appreciate that," Hannah said before she disappeared into the kitchen. The friends bowed their heads and, in quiet voices, prayed. They even dared to ask God whether somehow it might be possible Hannah wouldn't have to work that night.

The meal continued in a more conventional fashion. When Hannah came around to see how they were getting on and handed them their separate checks, she asked, "Do I know you from another restaurant? From Buck's? I'm sure I must have met you before. I worked there for a few years. You seem so familiar to me."

> *"It's by your kindness. I remember you because you're kind to me."*

Shari said, "You've served us here a couple of times. Where is Bucks?"

"Over in Woodsbury. Are you sure we didn't meet there?"

The women all shook their heads. "No, we've never gone there."

Jo joked, "Well, you know how it is. Ladies of a certain age can start looking all the same."

Hannah swiftly placed her hand on Jo's arm. "No. It is *not* that. It's by your kindness. I remember you because you're kind to me." And off she went to process credit cards and tips.

26

Jo saw Hannah approach again and said, "We prayed for you."

Hannah's face held what looked like a combination of wonder, relief, and happiness. "You are not going to believe this. I don't have to work tonight. A large reservation canceled, and my manager asked if I wanted tonight off after all—and I don't have to work!"

The friends, filled with joy, congratulated her and thanked the Lord for his amazing and swift answer to prayer.

Just before Hannah sped off again, she reached into her pocket and, with a radiant smile, dropped a large handful of wrapped mints on the table.

Getting the Runaround

by Charlaine Martin

OH, NO! I thought, peddling my heart out as we cycled away from the small harbor town. *He's gonna leave me behind! My dating profile said my goal was to ride on bike trails, not that I was a seasoned cyclist.* Afraid I'd fall over on my date's touring bike, I didn't slow down or stop—I could barely touch the ground. Besides, I would've ridden mine if I had a rack to bring it. My midlife body was fit, but this ride tested me.

My heart pounded as I glanced back to see where he was. As we sped past some farms and a golf course, I wondered, *What did I get myself into, coming to Michigan to spend time with a man I barely know?* He'd come to meet me at my home in Ohio for a few weekend dates, but we mostly talked on the phone and texted. Internet dating can be risky, and I wasn't sure about him yet. Were we even "in like"?

Confessions

Boaz rode up beside me when we pulled into the school parking lot, where his van awaited us. "Wow! You're sure fast! I could barely keep up with you. I had no idea you could ride like *that*." Sweat beads glistened on our brows as we dismounted our bicycles, unfazed by the lakeside chill.

"Really?" I replied, shocked at his confession. "You said that you ride regularly, but I'm just beginning to ride the trails at home. I was worried I couldn't keep up with *you* and *you'd* leave *me* behind. Oh, by the way, this bike seat is *terrible*!" My bony backside screamed in pain.

This runner-cyclist's voice escalated as he defended his seat choice. "I'll have you know it's a premium seat!"

"My tailbone disagrees." Wobbly-legged, I helped Boaz load the bikes onto his rack, and we returned to his house. *This ride was probably a show-stopper*, I groaned to myself, expecting him to tell me, "We had a nice day together, but 'God bless you in your search.'"

It's worth getting to know him more.

He didn't hesitate about meeting for church the following morning, though. *Is he waiting to brush me off after lunch on Sunday?* I wondered.

To my surprise, Boaz asked me about our next get-together in Ohio after lunch.

Hmm. He's nice and didn't get upset with me. It's worth getting to know him more, I mused.

Here We Go 'Round the Block!

On another early visit with Boaz in Michigan, he asked, "Would you help me drop my car off at the repair shop?"

"Sure," I agreed, empathizing with his need for a second driver.

He cautiously drove the forty-five-minute route to the shop while I followed him. Unfortunately, several vehicles and red lights separated us about a mile from our destination. While I followed my GPS, he arrived at the dealership's shop and waited inside for me.

When I entered the large, old port city across the lake from Canada, I became confused by the quirky angled streets and my GPS directions. Finally, I spotted the dealership but not the repair shop.

When Boaz had wondered what happened to me since I couldn't have been far behind, he walked out into the parking lot, looking for me. He couldn't call my cell phone since the Canadian cell towers put it on roaming. I'd later learn that when he spotted my car, he ran along the sidewalk waving wildly, thinking I'd see him and pull in.

I drove past the corner, looking in the opposite direction of where Boaz stood trying to get my attention, and I turned at the next corner. Then, I turned down an alley and again didn't know he scrambled to catch me.

After circling around yet again, I decided to pull into the car sales lot to ask for help. When I walked inside, a salesperson greeted me, "How can I help you?"

"I'm supposed to meet my boyfriend at your service center." I wasn't sure about our status, but it answered his question.

"Oh, let me page him for you. What's his name?" the man asked.

"Boaz Martin."

"Boaz Martin, someone is waiting for you in our showroom."

Surely, the loudspeaker blaring his name into the city would get his attention. Suddenly, he came in the side door, huffing and puffing with sweat trickling down his face. I guessed he wasn't prepared for another run after his morning jog.

Comparing Views

"What happened?" he asked, peering at me with his hands on his hips. He gestured his route as he told me about his crazy chase. "Didn't you see me running on the sidewalk waving my arms? I've been chasing you for the past few trips around the block!"

"Oh, I'm so sorry. Some drivers cut me off, and I hit some red lights. I lost sight of you. And then, I couldn't find the service department. So, after driving around a few times, I decided to pull in to see if you were here," I explained, feeling horrible I had caused him so much trouble. *This man won't ever want to see me ever again.* My heart sank. *He's a really nice guy. Too bad. Sigh.*

"I know! I chased you several rounds. You seriously mean you didn't see me running after your car?" he chuckled with a smirk. He'd neglected to tell me that trees and bushes had hidden the service building on a backlot behind the dealership. Playfully, he teased me for using my personal trainer skills to help him prep for his upcoming 5K race.

We laughed as tears streamed, comparing our versions of the story. Again, I wondered, *Is this date our last?* Boaz must have believed our relationship had merit, as we continued dating for another two years. His kind heart showed despite my blunders.

Dating Blunders End Beautifully

A friend once told me that dating when you're older is like kicking the tires of a used vehicle. We certainly "kicked each other's tires." What an amazing difference kindness makes in Christian dating and marriage. In Colossians 3:12–14, we read that Christian love displays compassion, kindness, humility, gentleness, and patience, which helps us forgive each other and unite us. When situations weren't ideal, we got a realistic view of each other's faults and Christian faith.

Before meeting each other, I'd hoped to find someone with the same loving-kindness as my late husband. Some of my early dates with others revealed self-centered interests in the midlife dating scene. If I had made these blunders with them, I would likely have been met with verbal jabs and ridicule. They lacked the genuine Christian love I sought.

It is loving-kindness that binds us together in unity. Genuine Christian love forms the foundation of a healthy Christian marriage.

Even after the shine of infatuation wore off in our remarriage, Christian kindness stands out with other fruit of the Spirit that drew us together. We certainly aren't perfect. Sparks have flown in arguments numerous times as iron sharpened iron.[5] We've often needed to forgive each other and ask forgiveness for hurts and our other human failings. But it is loving-kindness that binds us together in unity. Genuine Christian love forms the foundation of a healthy Christian marriage. Kindness that started during dating with lots of sweat and tears.

---

5. Proverbs 27:17

Glimmers on the Water

by Lisa-Anne Wooldridge

I LEANED MY HEAD back until water surrounded my face. As my feet floated up from beneath me, the gentle rocking of the warm, turquoise ocean lulled me into a dream-like state. The tension slowly left my body as the sun warmed my upturned face and illuminated the gentle wavelets around me. At long last, I was physically present in my "happy place."

Kindness Leads to Learning

When I was young, a sweet Sunday school teacher taught my class the fruit of the Spirit by way of a catchy song. I'm sure most of you would know the melody if I started to sing it, no matter how off-key. I was a two-church kid because my parents had different preferences, and I spent my growing years split between two denominations that couldn't have been more different.

One thing I noticed early on was the difference in Bible translations. They weren't the same! There were two lists of fruit and two different songs about them. Since the one church had a more rigid requirement of only using its preferred version, I cornered the pastor at the other church to explain why there were differences. Thankfully, he had a lot of time and grace for little girls with big questions.

I learned all about the history of the Bible and how it was translated over the centuries into different versions. When it came to the fruit of the Spirit, one word stuck out to me. It was rendered as *kindness* in one translation and *gentleness* in the other. I knew another verse where kindness was swapped with goodness in various versions—one that talks about how God's kindness *or* his goodness leads us to repentance.[6] I keep coming back to study kindness more in different languages and versions of the Bible. It's not as straightforward a word as it seems!

As with many "God-words," it's rich with extra nuance and meaning, brimming over with life breathed into it.

As with many "God-words," it's rich with extra nuance and meaning, brimming over with life breathed into it. In my mind, all the forms and functions of that word have melded together to mean a special sort of kindness—all wrapped up with God's love and goodness to us and his gentle benevolence toward us. Because of his kindness, I was currently toes-up under a blue sky in an azure sea that was the stuff of dreams.

Kindness Leads to Rest

It had been a difficult few years dealing with all the things you never want to deal with in life. As a result, my body was beat up, my brain was burned out, and my spirit was bone-dry. I dragged myself through each day because I had to, but I still took comfort in God's promises

---

6. Romans 2:4

that we'd never walk alone. I wasn't giving up on seeing the goodness of God in the land of the living.[7]

My husband—who is the epitome of a "keeper"—expressed concern about me and asked God for wisdom. During one of my lab appointments, he came with me to have my bloodwork done. I was a little anxious because my veins are not easy to draw from. I told the technician I was going to close my eyes and go to my happy place while she did her poking. Most nurses take that as a sign to be quiet and let the patient disassociate from what's happening, but I'd landed a very chatty one who insisted I tell her all about my favorite mental vacation.

As she worked, I described the soft sand and barely believable blue water of a Caribbean beach. My mind always went to the place I'd seen in a travel magazine but never hoped to visit. Our circumstances were such that even a weekend trip somewhere local was out of the question, but there are no travel restrictions on imagination. I just knew I could sink deeply into a healing rest if I was there. I didn't know yet that my sweet husband was already packing my suitcase in his mind while asking God for a way to get me there.

Kindness Leads to Refreshment

It was such a busy season of life for us, between children, ministry roles, and work. Dealing with health issues drained my battery faster than I could recharge it. My husband worked long hours on a project for his boss, and I worried he was becoming just as worn out. I missed spending time with him, especially time where we had the headspace to have a whole conversation and connect on a deeper level. He was always taking care of our family and me and generously giving from his time, energy, and resources to everyone around him. I longed for him to be refreshed the way he refreshed others.[8]

---

7. Psalm 27:13
8. Proverbs 11:25

I didn't know that God was already on the case, putting his plan into motion before we asked. For his hard work, my husband won an award and a bonus, and his boss strongly suggested he use it for a vacation. He used the words *rest, recharge,* and *relax*! They wanted him to come back refreshed. We wanted that for each other too. In fact, we both felt a little desperate to make it happen for the other one, which is how our miracle trip was planned in a matter of hours.

> *God was already on the case, putting his plan into motion before we asked.*

Things came together fast. A wonderful aunt called and offered to come stay with our children. I received an email telling me I'd been awarded enough free points to stay at a nice hotel the night before our ship was set to sail. My "good" bathing suit mysteriously showed up from the depths of my chaotic closet. At that point, I told God he was just showing off! But he knew how very much we needed a time of refreshing. I'm convinced we were headed for a complete crash otherwise.

Kindness Leads to Reflection

"What does it say?" My husband, who doesn't swim, stood waist-deep a few feet from where I floated. I was transfixed by the light dancing on the water and reflecting on the sandy ocean floor. I'd been staring at the patterns for a while, trying to etch the experience deep in my memory. The light weaving in and out with the movement of the water always enchanted me. It was nature's handwriting, and I always tried to decipher it.

"It says, 'Come to me when you're exhausted and worn out. I will help you put down your heavy burdens. I will give your soul rest.

Times of refreshing are found in my presence. No matter what troubles you walk through, I will revive you. I will restore your soul and give you new life.'"[9]

"It says all that?"

"All that and more. No matter where we are, he's our happy place, and when the world is overwhelming, he's our strong tower, our refuge, and his face shines on us even in the darkest days."

---

9. Matthew 11:28–30

If your gift is serving others, serve them well. If you are a teacher, teach well. If your gift is to encourage others, be encouraging. If it is giving, give generously. If God has given you leadership ability, take the responsibility seriously. And if you have a gift for showing kindness to others, do it gladly. Don't just pretend to love others. Really love them. Hate what is wrong. Hold tightly to what is good.

Romans 12:7–9 (nlt)

Sharing the Unbearable

by Joni Topper

"ARE YOU ALONE? Where are you?" My sister's voice quivered on the phone. This was not a great way to start a conversation. The message got harder from there. Is there a gentle way to share a message of loss? My beloved sister explained that her son, my nephew, had succumbed to the mental illness and addictions that haunted him for years. "Walter just took his life," she cried.

Walter had served a ten-year prison sentence that ended last summer. His attempts to find stability since then had left him miserable. Reentering society is always hard after that kind of a sentence, but when mental illness is present, the challenges multiply.

Many people prayed for him, believed for him, and loved him throughout his journey. He was part of a tight-knit family who fought their way through losses and disappointments and the trials of life with victory, joy, and purpose. We could do this because of our faith. We know this life is not all there is. There's so much more.

Walter was not born into a group of people who gave up on him. He was not denied an education. He had the privilege of growing up in a middle-class family in the richest country in the world. Still, there was a heaviness in him.

> *We could do this because of our faith....*
> *this life is not all there is.*

He made a profession of his faith in Jesus as his Savior as a young man. He shared his testimony in public. He was not always without hope.

When this life-changing phone call came, I was on the floor putting a piece of furniture together for my grandson. At eighteen years old, he was able to purchase a small house. That day, he became a homeowner. It was moving day. The day was full of excitement and promise for him. I finished helping him and then drove an hour back home.

Not the First Time

As I drove home to pack and head to my sister's, I recalled the day I went back to work after the death of my *other* sister's daughter many years ago. Now, both of my siblings had lost a child. It was unthinkable to me. My niece died at age thirteen. And my nephew was gone at forty.

When Kerri died, I remember walking across the post office parking lot headed to work at 6:00 a.m. a day or so after her funeral. Dread filled me. My heart cried out, "Please, stop time for a while." I needed to be still. Just stop. "Stop and let me catch my breath before going back to the regular world. I'm not ready." My pleas to God did not produce any help in that moment.

I sucked in a deep breath, determined not to cry, then pushed through the chained door onto the workroom floor. When she heard the chains pull through the door, my coworker looked up with delight on her face. "My first grandbaby was born last night! As soon as we get this mail up, I'm leaving here and heading that direction."

Scripture raced through my numb mind. Something about "to everything there is a season."[10] As I drew in one more deep breath, my heart knew that the season had just shifted. With one foot still in grief and disbelief, I needed to step the other into wonder and delight with my friend and celebrate her precious grandchild. This moment was about her wonderful season. What kind of a friend would I be to not celebrate with her? The emotion she was experiencing could not have been more opposite than my personal state of mind. Still, both were valid. I chose to celebrate with her.

Pack and Go

Pulling under the carport, I snapped back to today. How can this be? Here I am again, experiencing a joyous life moment marked by an unimaginable tragedy. "Pack a bag, Joni. Get back in the car and get to your sister's house as quickly as possible. You need to be there, and she needs you to be there." My self-talk propelled me through the necessary tasks.

The next few days were filled with people, greetings, sifting through pictures, family stories, and togetherness. The fruit we talked about at church—goodness, gentleness, kindness, and faithfulness were on display. All around us, there was a spirit of cooperation. One of us sisters was good at this. So, she took care of this. One of us was good at that. She took care of that. It was like the most sacred tender space, and we were together. Kindness ruled every moment.

The morning of the funeral, my sister whose son died went to church with me a couple of hours before the service. I sat at the piano and played and sang. She sang with me. The songs that are always a blessing were more than that now. They were a balm. Scriptures filled

---

10. Ecclesiastes 3:1

the air with the very kindness of God. "The LORD bless you and keep you; the LORD make his face to shine upon you and be gracious to you."[11]

Life Goes On

A few days into this experience, my sister said, "I've been grieving him for years throughout his struggles. I feel like David in the Bible when his son was dying. He would not eat or get up until the child died. Then he arose immediately and ate and went back to living a life of joy, knowing that God in his sovereignty had answered his prayer. He took the child home."[12]

"All the bases have been covered," she said. "I am so thankful for all the people around me. I did not have to do anything. I couldn't do anything, and I did not need to. This kindness that surrounded me in the form of the body of Christ took care of everything." My brother-in-law sat by my sister, sipping his coffee as we shared this conversation just ten days after my nephew passed. He commented with a giggle, "You're still not doing anything."

Kindness shifts the impact of unbearable moments and makes them shareable.

God's provision in this life event was like a rolling flood. It came in one wave after another with just enough force to enable us all to stand. That Bible verse kept happening, the one about being kind and tenderhearted toward one another.[13] As though the script was being

---

11. Numbers 6:24–25 (ESV)
12. 2 Samual 12:16–23
13. Ephesians 4:32

played out in front of us, we were shown what this looks like in real life, and it was much more beautiful than any of us could have imagined.

I cannot explain how days of grief over such a tragedy ended in such comfort and peace. It's true, though. While we continue to process all that happened, the presence of our God still fills the moments with a keen awareness of his kindness. Kindness shifts the impact of unbearable moments and makes them shareable.

Kindling Kindness

by Carolyn Gaston

She opens her mouth in wisdom, and the teaching of kindness is on her tongue.

PROVERBS 31:26 (ESV)

"IF YOU'RE A kind person, you're not mean, and you use a sweet voice," answered my six-year-old granddaughter when I asked her what it meant to be kind. I chuckled when she said, "If you help an old lady get up out of her chair, you are kind." I wondered if she was thinking about me. She concluded her definition with these wise words. "When you open the door for someone and smile at them, it lets them know you saw them and they deserved your smile."

I'm very happy that my granddaughter understands the basics of being kind. I would love to help her set a goal to be kind as she grows up. My prayer is that she will answer the question, "What do you want to be when you grow up?" with one word: "KIND!"

Teaching

I am not a kind person by nature and cannot become a kinder person by simply drifting through my days. I must be very deliberate and do kind things on purpose. Not only do I want to be kind in the things I do and say but also to teach my kids and grandkids the art of kindness. As a teacher by trade, I may tend to be academic and straightforward and just provide them with a how-to of kind acts. If given a list of kind things to say to others, children learn ways to speak kindly. I want to encourage them to look for kindness all around them instead of focusing on negative things.

"If you're a kind person, you're not mean, and you use a sweet voice."

The Bible contains a plethora of verses about kindness that we can memorize. For example, Ephesians teaches us to be kind, compassionate, and forgiving, like God.[14] The Old Testament instructs us to post God's commands in our homes.[15] A practical way to implement this would be to hang framed Scriptures or catchy quotes on our walls. These displays can provide valuable teaching moments for our young ones, as well as remind us of the truths of God's Word. Of course, the most important example I can show my children is Jesus Christ, who is the epitome of kindness and compassion.

One kind gesture we can teach children is to write heartfelt thank-you notes. I may have to provide specific words and phrases to get them started, but this is a good way to pass on the dying art of letter writing to the next generation.

---

14. Ephesians 4:32
15. Deuteronomy 6:9

Storytelling

Another way to teach kindness is by telling stories that demonstrate that trait. God taught the Israelites to pass down their traditions by telling their children about the mighty works he had done in the past.[16] I like to read those Bible stories to my kids and grandkids and also to share with them the many ways God has been kind to me and to our family.

Kind acts may seem sent from God and can possibly change the trajectory of your life.

I recently asked some friends to tell me the kindest thing anyone ever did for them. Within the variety of beautiful stories shared with me, the following truths emerged:

- We need to be on the lookout for people in need.
- Kind acts may seem sent from God and can possibly change the trajectory of your life.
- A kind act can bring comfort and even rescue you in an emergency.
- Doing kind deeds takes time and sacrifice and demonstrates generosity and giving.
- Kindness can be paid forward.

Modeling

A less obvious but impactful method of teaching kindness is modeling. It is my hope that when my kids see me offer a helping hand to a stranger, it will prompt them to do the same someday. When they hear me compliment a neighbor, it sets an example for them to do likewise

---

16. Psalm 78:4–7

in the future. Generously tipping a waitress gives them an illustration of kindness. If I make a habit of checking in on people who are sick or vulnerable, this models a pattern for my kids about caring for others.

Since giving humble, merciful kindness does not come easy for me, I have to remind myself every day to be an intentional example. I pray that when my kids see me doing kind deeds, this will kindle kindness in their hearts, and they will find opportunities to be thoughtful. I also hope they realize we do acts of kindness without expecting anything in return or bragging about what we've done.

Timing

The book of Proverbs teaches us that when we have the power to do something good, we should do it.[17] It is my prayer to live by this truth and train my children to do the same. In Galatians, we are instructed to do good to all people when we have the opportunity.[18] These words motivate me to be on the lookout each day for specific opportunities to show someone I care by being kind since those situations may never present themselves again.

To help reinforce the idea of looking for opportunities, I could challenge my kids to do one kind deed every day for a month and have them challenge me to do the same. What a tangible way to hold each other accountable for being kinder people!

Targeting

I have learned that when I want to do a good deed for someone, I may need to ask them first and not just assume I know what they need. Years ago, I thought some friends of mine who lived in a trailer park needed me to get their landlord to fix all the holes in their driveway. However, when I mentioned my idea to them, they told me what they

---

17. Proverbs 3:27
18. Galatians 6:10

really needed was better lighting outside so their kids would be safer at night. Thankfully, they spoke up and clearly stated their need to me, so my kind act was on target.

It is important to stay in touch with people and groups who are already doing good things on a regular basis. Tell them what your skillset is and what you have a passion for. Who knows? One of us may be just the person they need for their next project.

Blessing

Kindness makes the world a better place and makes us better people. One kind deed can often lead to another. By his Holy Spirit, God can use us to bless others through acts of kindness.

By his Holy Spirit, God can use us to bless others through acts of kindness.

Scientific studies have shown that being kind to others has biological benefits. It can increase self-esteem, empathy, and compassion. It can decrease blood pressure and cortisol and reduce stress. It can also reduce loneliness, improve mood, and produce feelings of happiness.[19] Let's be courageous, get out of our comfort zones, and do kind things! This is how the children learn kindness.

---

[19]. Sarah Strahm, CNP, APNP, "Kindness in Action Brings Healthy Rewards," Mayo Clinic Health System, January 27, 2022, accessed February 21, 2025, https://www.mayoclinichealthsystem.org/hometown-health/speaking-of-health/kindness-in-action-brings-healthy-rewards.

A Little Kindness Goes Far

by Diana Leagh Matthews

So then, as we have opportunity, let us do good to everyone, and especially to those who are of the household of faith.

GALATIANS 6:10 (ESV)

A STRANGER INTERRUPTED OUR party in the best way possible. I've never forgotten his kindness, even though it happened years ago. He saw a need and wanted to help a young boy have the best birthday ever. He gave above and beyond anything we expected.

It all started when Mama, my grandmother, and I joined my sister and her family to celebrate my oldest nephew's birthday. He was about to turn five years old.

This was a joint birthday celebration, as Jacob was born three days after my grandmother's eightieth birthday, and she was tickled to share her birthday with her great-grandson.

GATHER THE GOODNESS

As we sat around the table at Cracker Barrel and visited, we reflected on the upcoming changes in my sister's family. Jacob had just become a big brother three months earlier.

However, the roughest challenge lay ahead. My brother-in-law would ship out to Afghanistan the following weekend for his second tour of duty. He'd served for over a year in Iraq when Jacob was a baby.

Our hearts were heavy as we prayed for Shannon's safety while overseas. Being a mom to two little boys isn't easy, but it's even more of a challenge when you're parenting alone. Even given our two-hour distance, we'd do what we could to help my sister and her family.

While we were eating, a man came over to our table. I don't remember what drew him over, but it may have been Shannon's army fatigues. The stranger thanked Shannon for his service.

As the men talked, they discussed Jacob's birthday and Shannon's upcoming deployment. Then the stranger reached into his pocket, pulled out a bill, and handed it to Jacob.

He said something along the lines of, "Here you go, young man. A little something for your birthday." Then he was gone.

When Jacob opened his hand to look at the gift, he saw the man had handed him a $50 bill.

"What are you going to do with your money?" someone asked the child.

We never know the difference we may make in a person's life.

"Put it in the bank and save it." Jacob surprised and delighted us all with his pronouncement.

A little bit of kindness can go a long way. This stranger's kindness lifted a little boy's mood and reminded him that people cared and that his father was making a difference through his service.

It's a reminder to reach out to others and give what we have. No matter how little or much that might be. We never know the difference we may make in a person's life.

God, thank you for the reminder to approach others with kindness. Help me to give what I have, whether it's a kind word, a helping hand, or a financial gift. May others see you through my words and actions.

Goodness

When Goodness Passes By

by Kolleen Lucariello

"DID YOU SEE that?"

Raising my eyes, I hoped to catch a glimpse of whatever my chauffeur-husband was pointing out. "See what?" I asked.

"Never mind. You missed it. You weren't looking."

Because we have family and friends spread throughout the states, this conversation repeats countless times during the many hours we've spent traveling the road together. I'd missed it—again.

Distractions, Detours, and Defining Moments

Often, I'm too distracted to catch whatever noteworthy sight he hopes I will see. The scrolling on my phone absorbs my attention, or my fingers are tapping away on my laptop. My nose might be buried in a book, or sometimes I'm just napping. Inevitably, I miss some pretty amazing things because my focus is on something else. It's nearly impossible to notice everything when we're speeding down the highway, but my husband has learned not to assume I won't need a stop at the

GATHER THE GOODNESS

rest area just because I haven't asked. He now anticipates the answer will be, "Yes, please," when, or if, he notices a rest stop approaching—because I'll be too distracted.

While reading through the book of Exodus, I hit the brakes and paused for a moment when I noticed a question Moses asked God. It seemed to jump right out in front of me. Moses and the Israelites were making their way through the wilderness to the land God had promised to give them. Leaving Egypt wasn't exactly a smooth transition, and the journey had proven to be rather bumpy.

I miss some pretty amazing things because my focus is on something else.

When the Israelites inaccurately assumed Moses, and therefore, God, had abandoned them, they reverted to habits learned from their days in Egypt—they made a god out of gold. A definite lapse of judgment became a crucial moment of decision between Israel, Moses, and God. If Moses hadn't interceded on behalf of the Israelites, God might have followed through with his threat to end the relationship. Thank goodness for intercessors who stand in the gap for one another.

After a conversation with God, Moses boldly asked, "Please show me your glory." In response, God assured him, "I will make all my goodness pass before you and will proclaim before you my name 'The Lord.' And I will be gracious to whom I will be gracious, and will show mercy on whom I will show mercy."[20]

Moses asked to see God's glory, and in response, God revealed that his glory would be seen in his goodness. God continually sought to show his glory through his abundant goodness to the Israelites, but

---

20. Exodus 33:19 (ESV)

they would need to stop allowing the gods of Egypt to distract them from noticing it. Relatable? Absolutely.

When God's Goodness Passes Unnoticed

After years of traveling down the same road, my husband and I found it a bit humorous one day to realize we'd become oblivious to the fact that a new building stood where a house once did. We'd never noticed when the house went missing from where it once stood so stately. Life can become so habitual that it's easy to overlook what's right in front of us—or, should I say, was right there.

Likewise, a smorgasbord of daily distractions obstructs our view, hindering our ability to notice God's goodness as it passes by. I can't help but wonder how often I ask God to reveal his glory yet fail to truly look for his goodness in my not-so-good moments.

When our brother-in-law was killed in a car accident, I was so angry that God would allow this tragedy to happen. I asked, "Where were you, God?" and blamed him.

Then, his goodness passed by through the words of the officiating pastor. "You might be asking," he said, "'Where were you, God, when Brad died?' and I am here to tell you God was in the same place he was when his Son died."

I didn't recognize it then, but now I see how God's goodness passed by through his compassionate care and patience for me while I was hot with anger toward him.

Years later, in fact, almost to the day, we suffered the loss of a dear friend in another car accident. Grief struck again, and I cried out, "God, show me where you are in this." And once more, his goodness passed by—this time through the celebration of a life devoted to Jesus, reflected in a funeral filled with love, faith, and the hope of eternity.

I wish I could say I always ask God to show me his glory during seasons of pain. I've been blindsided by the crushing weight of grief—losing a sister and dear friends I had fervently believed he would restore to health. The sting of sickness, the burden of regret, and the relentless echo of defeat can make it hard to lift our eyes and ask God to show us his glory. Hard seasons may make it difficult to recognize his goodness as it passes by, but that doesn't mean he is absent. God promises to be "our refuge and strength, a very present help in trouble,"[21] but often, in our troubles, we become distracted by the voice that would forever want to discredit him.

When we struggle to trust God, we fail to see where and how his goodness is moving in our lives. Instead of acknowledging that he is the source of our blessings, we credit luck, coincidence, or our own efforts. Yet, how quickly we blame him when troubles arise.

Fear and stress are huge distractors fighting for my focus. I must become intentional to ask God to show me his glory in every season and situation. Hope is restored when I remember how I've seen his goodness pass by through previous blessings and provision.

The constant distraction of a digital life lures me into comparison and envy, distancing me from contentment. Before the days of social media, I might have envied a friend's new car, but I wasn't bombarded with reminders of everything I was missing. The more I fixate on what others have, the less I recognize God's goodness in my life. The noise of a curated online world will drown out the quiet moments when God's goodness passes by, and I find my worth and identity in him alone.

Gathering His Goodness

After describing the fruit of the Spirit, Paul urged the Galatian church to "keep in step with the Spirit."[22] But how can I keep up if unbelief holds me back or if I resist adjusting to life's challenges by taking the

---

21. Psalm 46:1 (ESV)
22. Galatians 5:25 (ESV)

necessary steps of faith? Just as we gather fruit in a basket for nourishment, gathering God's goodness provides the spiritual sustenance that strengthens our trust in him—especially in difficult seasons.

How often has God's goodness passed by unnoticed because your focus was elsewhere?

When I reconcile myself to my identity in Christ and seek his kingdom perspective, I become less distracted by the noise around me and more attuned to his presence.

How often has God's goodness passed by unnoticed because your focus was elsewhere? Perhaps it's time to let him fill your basket.

Goodness and Merci

by Lisa-Anne Wooldridge

MERCI FORD SAT in the bed of her dad's old truck, picking at the rusty paint with her fingernail. There was no moon, but the stars, like diamonds on black velvet in the sky, cast all the light she needed. Curled up under her grandmother's quilt with the dog she'd inherited from her older brother, Merci felt surrounded by the family she might never see again.

She'd been up on the mountain when the skies broke open. The Maddox baby had chosen that night to come into the world, never mind what the weather man said about it being a good time to stay home. She was the only student midwife available to go. She'd taken her dad's pickup in case the narrow mountain tracks slicked up or washed out, and though it was as old as her father, the truck was just as reliable. The weatherman was right, though. There'd been a gully washer to beat all. She counted backward and realized the baby had been born a full two days ago. Her father's pickup had become her temporary shelter.

She could hear the black water rushing and scraping its way down the face of the mountain, pouring into the valley below. It hadn't been so bad, she thought, when she'd set out for home. She was tired, and her own soft bed was calling her name. The old-timers, though, gathered at the little cabin for the birth, had sworn they'd never seen the like and were afraid to let her go. In one corner, the granny rocked the new baby and mumbled about the end of days. They'd let Merci leave only under protest.

Colleen Maddox, the matriarch of the clan, had spoken plainly to her.

"If'n you can stand what we got, we'd be proud to have ya stay with us, Merci. Yer folks wouldn't want you out on the road. No tellin' what could happen, and if sumpin' got hold o'ya, or the water carried ya off, I don't want it said that we turned ya out."

Merci warmed at the generous offer. She knew mountain hospitality was always earnest and heartfelt. "No, you never would turn a body out, ma'am. But I got to get back. If things are bad down below, Mama and Daddy might get stranded and need the truck. Don't worry about me. I know every track and deer trail down the mountain. I'll be just fine." Merci gave the woman a bright smile to reassure her. "You just enjoy that baby and take care of Delia-Rose for me. She did so good, but it took a lot out of her."

Now, though, stranded as she was, she wished she hadn't been so sure of herself. *Always getting myself into trouble.* She flicked paint chips away. It was a good thing Bo had come along for the ride. He wasn't much of a hunting dog, but he'd scared off a mountain lion the night before with his impressive bark. Even with Bo's protective nature and the warmth he shared with her, she couldn't fall asleep.

She wrestled with different solutions. Abandon the truck and find a place to cross the angry water by foot or circle around the mountain in hopes of finding an undamaged house? The truth was, though, she could do nothing in the dangerous dark but wait. Driving uphill was not an option. The narrow track she'd been traveling on had given way, collapsing out from under her. The old Chevy truck was carried down by a landslide and came to rest in the mud on a slender bank. She was just feet from the swollen Little Sugar Creek, where she'd been stuck ever since.

A tear slipped down her face. She'd never felt so helpless, hungry, or tired, but it was the fear that kept her awake. If the water rose any higher, she knew she could be swept away from her precarious perch. The daylight hours had passed, with the churned-up water running fast and full of debris. It wouldn't end well if she were to get pulled into that current. She looked up at the stars and couldn't look away. They were beautiful, so unbelievably lovely, but very far away. *Kind of like you, God*, she thought, even though it triggered an internal alarm. She knew better, but yet, there it was. She felt abandoned by the Almighty. She believed in the goodness of God, but it sure seemed a long way off.

Merci stared at the stars until she felt as if she were falling upward, into the heavens, swept away not by the churning black water but by an invisible current carrying her somewhere far from earth. She closed her eyes, longing for sleep, but the swirling inside kept jolting her awake. She was a little girl again, lost, alone, and afraid.

It was then that she heard the voice. Try as she might, she couldn't open her eyes. It was a woman's voice, strong and rich and full of living, with a distinctive mountain lilt. It carried down the mountain, brushing the laurel bushes and the rhododendrons on the way. She was singing familiar words set to the tune of an old mountain ballad. It sounded mournful, but the words were full of hope.

"Though weepin' may spend th' night, 'tis joy that comes in th' mornin' light. Hold on to hope with all your might. Goodness an' joy come with the mornin' light . . ."

The words were like a lullaby, soothing and caressing her anxious heart. She soon sighed and gave up the fight. Come what may, she would rest in the goodness of God. In the cold, on the too-firm bed of an old truck, even though she was inches away from certain death, she would rest.

A soft wind stirred as she slept, and in those night hours, the rushing torrent ran its course. Much of the water was siphoned off into limestone caves and underground rivers. A rich deposit of topsoil was left in the valley, and a large white stone of gleaming bedrock was scrubbed clear in the bed of Little Sugar Creek. It was just wide enough for one old Chevy truck to cross on solid ground. It carved a way out of the wilderness where there was none before. "I have seen the goodness of the Lord," she said to her happy, tail-wagging pup, "in the land of the living."

Merci Ford drove her dad's Chevy down the mountain that day, but her faith soared to new heights—maybe even to the stars.

Marvelous Mosaics

by Carolyn Gaston

Casting all your anxieties on him, because he cares for you.
1 Peter 5:7 (ESV)

Dear God, thank you that I can cast
    all my anxiety on you,
Knowing that you care about everything
    I'm going through.
As I write this prayer, guide me with your Holy Spirit
So that my words will glorify you
And bring hope and joy.

Lord, will you change my perspective on hard times?
Stir my heart to know you see me
And your hand is on me, working for my good.
Help me see hardships as pieces of the mosaic
You are creating for your glory.

Help me accept that it's a process,
But your goodness is coming,
Following after me all the days of my life.

Trusting that your goodness is waiting on
    the other side of my struggles
Brings me hope and assurance
And the will to keep going.
You have given me thousands of
    promises in your Word
To cling to as I wait for peace.

Peace will come when I realize you are a good God,
No matter what the circumstances,
No matter how much evil I see around me,
No matter how much my heart aches,
No matter how many mistakes I make.

Help me accept that it's a process,
But your goodness is coming,
Following after me all the days of my life.

Even when I'm sad, angry, and confused,
I will refuse to be bitter; I want to be better.
Help me move forward one step at a time,
Knowing that you are shaping my character,
Making me more like Jesus.

I can believe in your faithfulness
Because my story isn't over.
You can use it to help others,
Weave our stories together,
Bringing good out of bad.

Help me to see that it's a process,
But your goodness is coming,
Following after me all the days of my life.

I know you are with me even in my darkest days.
As the waves of worry roar around me,
Remind me you will never leave me.
You will get me through the storm,
And I will be stronger on the other side.

Use me to bring light to others,
To pour faith into their fears,
Hope into their hopelessness,
And peace into their pain
So they can lean into your loving-kindness.

Help me see that it's a process,
But your goodness is coming,
Following after me all the days of my life.

As I pour out my feelings to you,
I believe you are with me
In my mess, in my mistakes, in my misery.
Help me see with eyes of faith, not fear.
You are my faithful Father.

GATHER THE GOODNESS

I will be still and know that you are
    my God and you are good.
Recognizing your abundant goodness
Brings me security in the storms,
Hope in the hardships,
And comfort in the chaos.

Help me see that it's a process,
But your goodness is coming,
Following after me all the days of my life.

You are bringing good from bad,
Creating a marvelous mosaic
Arranged gently by your strong hand.
A story of the fears and failures, of doubt and despair,
A unique masterpiece for your glory.

I know that I am not the only one suffering.
Give me the assurance that you will
    use my personal pain
In a way that you can use no one else's.
From the depths of my hurting heart,
    out of my current sorrow,
May my song rise up to glorify you and
    draw others to your grace.

Help me see that it's a process,
But your goodness is coming,
Following after me all the days of my life.

The Lost Bike

by Victoria Hanan Romo

TOMMY, A "CRADLE Catholic," wasn't the likeliest candidate for a budding atheist. Despite being the recipient of multiple church sacraments—baptism, first communion, confession—he was, at the tender age of ten, already wrestling with God's existence.

Seeds of doubt were first planted at the church's teaching that unbaptized babies couldn't go to heaven. *How*, Tommy thought, *is that fair? And if that isn't true, maybe the whole God thing isn't true either.* Tommy never had any personal encounter to convince him otherwise. His home life taught him not to expect a great deal, including from God.

Enter the Bike

It wasn't much—the used black Schwinn was too big and a hand-me-down from his father's friend. But it was his. Tommy hadn't thought it a big deal when he got it, but over time, he began to like it. He went on long rides, doing daredevil stunts that would have horrified his parents. It was fun to challenge his limits.

One day, as he plotted his next death-defying feat, he was surprised to find the bike gone. Figuring it would come up—theft was almost unheard of in their modest, working-class neighborhood—he was disappointed when the bike remained missing. It had been a couple of days already.

Tommy, a stoic, didn't cry. He was used to going without. Still, he missed it. Then the thought hit him: *This might be the perfect test to see whether God is real.*

Tommy didn't put much stock in prayer. His school taught that God may or may not answer his prayers. What was the point then? Even so, he tried. His impersonal heavenly entreaties consisted of praying for the poor or world peace. It seemed selfish and wrong to pray for his own needs.

This time, however, he would give it a shot. The prayer was more of a challenge, and Tommy knew he had to get it right. That night in bed, he thought of ways to test God. Tommy considered a few scenarios, but none satisfied him. *His* test was going to be hard. Almost impossible.

Finally, he had it.

Let the Games Begin

"God," he prayed, "If you're real, I want to get my bike in the next ten minutes. I want it now, not tomorrow."

Tommy chuckled. It wasn't a realistic ask. It was already approaching midnight. In the mid-1960s—when this story happened—it was simply unheard of to call anyone after 9:00 p.m. Still, he lay in his bed and waited, watching the clock with zero expectation. One minute ticked by. Then another.

To Tommy's utter astonishment, the phone rang! The heavy rotary phone vibrated with the loud rings, waking the entire household. Tommy's father shouted for him to answer it.

Tommy gingerly approached the phone. It was the family's first late-night call, and it shattered the peace like a hammer on glass. He tried to calm his galloping heart. It was probably a wrong number.

"Hello," he managed. To Tommy's shock, it was his best friend! Stevie's voice was hesitant.

"Hey, I'm sorry I called so late," he practically choked. "I don't know why, but I woke up and just had to call you! I had to tell you that your bike is down here—on the side of the garage." Stevie apologized over and over.

Tommy reassured him. "It's okay, buddy. Thanks for calling me." Tommy couldn't stop the goosebumps erupting all over his body as he hung up. *God*, he thought, *made Stevie call! God!* He stared out the window in wonder. Stars twinkled in the distance. The moon was full and bright. Tommy always liked space. One of his few joys in life was watching *Star Trek* on Thursday nights. It was weird to think that God, who made the whole universe, knew *him*—little Tommy James Sullivan! A nobody from nowhere special. Dayton, Ohio, wasn't exactly the Riviera. Not only that, but God cared enough to give him his bike back.

He reached out to heaven again, this time with an olive branch. "Well, God," he conceded, "you're real, and I'm sorry for doubting you."

Tommy has been believing ever since.

☙❧

Grace and God's Goodness

God spoke through Isaiah, "I will answer them before they even call to me. While they are still talking about their needs, I will go ahead and answer their prayers!"[23]

---

23. Isaiah 65:24 (NLT)

GATHER THE GOODNESS

Tommy lost his bike—and found life-changing faith. Such is grace!

God's grace is likely the ultimate manifestation of his goodness. Defined as "unmerited favor" by the early church fathers, grace is effectively how God, in his sweetness, reaches out to the doubting Tommy in all of us.

God's grace is likely the ultimate manifestation of his goodness.

"Come touch," he seems to say as he guides our fingers toward his nail-scarred hand as Jesus did for Thomas, the apostle who initially doubted his resurrection.[24] "Come see," he continues, inviting us to observe the loveliness of creation. Repeatedly, he urges us to hear his voice—the promptings of the Holy Spirit. Prayer is described as sweet-smelling incense that ushers in the presence of God.[25] Ultimately engaging all our senses, he exhorts us, "Come taste and see that the Lord is good."[26] We are invited to partake in communion, to literally consume his goodness and make it our own!

In all of it, the Lord seems to be saying, bottom line, "Can't you see how much I love you?"

The goodness of grace is perhaps best embodied by the experience of the thief on the cross. As an eyewitness to Jesus's patient endurance in the face of extraordinary injustice, even forgiving and praying for his tormentors, the thief's heart softened. Faith was born. His own life, he realized, stood in stark contrast to the Lord's goodness. All too aware of the depth of his misdeeds and their just consequences, he reached out

---

24. John 20:24–29
25. Psalm 141:2
26. Psalm 34:8 (NLT)

in humility and truth. "Jesus," he begged, "Remember me when you come into your Kingdom."

Grace responded. "And Jesus replied, "I assure you, today you will be with me in paradise."[27] Surely, the thief's final moments were filled with total peace—and joyous anticipation of the life to come.

It is grace that leads us to faith. Whether, like Tommy, we face the everyday erosion of circumstances from without or, like the thief, come to the searing realization of our own sin from within, God meets us where we're at. This is grace. The Lord seeks not only to expand our faith to believe him for salvation but also trust him to daily make us more like Jesus.

REFLECTION

Have you ever received grace—God's gracious goodness—in the face of unbelief? How did that affect your walk with God? How can you share that same grace with others today?

> *Heavenly Father, thank you for receiving me even when I, a full-grown doubting Thomas, was blind to your presence. Help me to know you better, especially in testing and trials, and to cry, like the father in the Gospel story, "I do believe, but help me overcome my unbelief!"*[28]

---

27. Luke 23:42–43 (NLT)
28. Mark 9:24 (NLT)

Learn to do good.
Seek justice.
Help the oppressed.
Defend the cause of orphans.
Fight for the rights of widows.

Isaiah 1:17 (NLT)

The Winding Trail

by Sally Ferguson

ON THE LEFT, massive sea grape bushes brushed against our shoulders. On the right, coral crags jutted out against the blue waters of the Pacific Ocean. The waves splashed up as the coral and sand crunched beneath our feet. It was the most beautiful feeling to listen to the Hawaiian surf pummel the shore and taste the salty air. Hubby and I continued our trek toward supper.

"The restaurant is a short jaunt from our lodging," they said. "It offers unique island flair," they said. "They" were strangers to us but friends on an adventure, so onward we went. We watched the sun dip behind the horizon and marveled at its luminescent rays. We took pictures along the way to preserve the moment. Eventually, the phone became our flashlight, illuminating the path for one then shining it back for the other. And then, the trail disappeared.

Stranded and Lost

Have you ever set out on what you believed was where you were meant to be, only to feel stranded along the way? Maybe you began your business with high hopes, and things didn't take off like you thought they would? We know the verse: "Your word is a lamp to my feet and a light to my path."[29] But sometimes it feels as if the light has gone out.

Let's take a look at the widow of Zarephath.[30] She had hit upon hard times. When the prophet Elijah found her, she was down to her last meal. God sent Elijah to her rescue with instructions to supply him with food. She also provided a room for Elijah during a drought. But one day, the widow's son died. Oh, how she mourned. She must have felt the darkness close in. She was doing God's will yet experienced the unthinkable.

God is at work behind the scenes to raise your heart from despair and to bring glory to his name.

Have you wondered where God went when your path grew dim? "For You are my lamp, O Lord; The Lord shall enlighten my darkness."[31]

Back to the Dark Path

Meanwhile, our path on the Big Island had grown cold. We could see twinkling lights across the bay but thought it couldn't be our destination—it was too far away. We climbed up on the jagged coral and lava rocks to see where the trail was, then backtracked to try another route. It was dark. It seemed hopeless.

Likewise, the widow's route seemed hopeless.

---

29. Psalm 119:105 (NKJV)
30. 1 Kings 17:7–24
31. 2 Samuel 22:29 (NKJV)

Does your way feel hopeless?
But God.[32]

Yes, we did arrive at our destination. Yes, Elijah raised the widow's son back to life. And, yes, God has a plan for you. It may seem hopeless, but don't lose hope. God is at work behind the scenes to raise your heart from despair and to bring glory to his name. He will set your feet on the right path once again.

"Suddenly, God, you floodlight my life; I'm blazing with glory, God's glory!"[33]

**What do you need God to do for you?
Will you ask a friend to pray on your behalf?**

Lord, when life throws me against the tide, help me to look to you for safety. It's scary to feel stranded, yet you continually remind me not to be afraid. I trust you to chase away the darkness.

---

32. Genesis 50:20
33. Psalm 18:28 (MSG)

Your awe-inspiring deeds will be on every tongue;
I will proclaim your greatness.
Everyone will share the story of your wonderful goodness;
they will sing with joy about your righteousness.
The Lord is merciful and compassionate,
slow to get angry and filled with unfailing love.

Psalm 145:6–8 (nlt)

Remember God's Goodness

by Dawn Marie Wilson

God is good, a hiding place in tough times. He recognizes and welcomes anyone looking for help, No matter how desperate the trouble.

Nahum 1:7–8 (msg)

THE PROPHET NAHUM proclaims, "God is good." Goodness is part of God's nature. His intentions and motives are always good, and that's important to remember when we're overwhelmed by troubles. Forgetting God's goodness will not help us. On the other hand, remembering God's goodness can assist us in dealing with terrible circumstances, even tragic events.

Shortly after my diagnosis with multiple myeloma in 2019, I wrote a tearful message on Facebook. "I would like to be healed," I said, "but I believe my Father God is using cancer to bring about a good and greater purpose. He is making me more like Jesus. Cancer is not good; it will never be good. But God is good, and all he does is good. If you are a Christian, look for God's goodness and loving purpose, no matter

GATHER THE GOODNESS

your circumstances. It is there. You may just be blinded temporarily by your tears."[34]

I'll admit that in my physical and emotional weakness, I had days when I fought hard to believe God is good. Satan certainly wants us to think God *is not* good. He wants us to proclaim that terrible lie amid our frustration, confusion, and suffering. But when we choose to remember the reality of God's goodness, we can thwart the impact of the Enemy's plans.

Consequences of Forgetting

Forgetting God's goodness is not only an insult to his grace—it has real-life consequences. We see examples of this in the lives of the Israelites during the Exodus. When they forgot God's goodness, they often played into Satan's hands.

God mercifully brought his people out of slavery in Egypt, but about six weeks later, they forgot God's goodness and grumbled about their troubles in the wilderness. They showed contempt for God's provision of manna from heaven. Instead, they idealized their wretched years of bondage and yearned for the garlic and onions of Egypt. Unbelievable selective memory! At one point, in their frustration, they thought it better to die as slaves under Pharaoh than trust God for the next steps of their journey. They were not mindful of God's protection and guidance through the desert with a pillar of cloud by day and a pillar of fire by night.

The Israelites experienced miracle after miracle—bitter waters made sweet, water from a rock, and winds bringing quail. God even kept their clothes and sandals from wearing out for forty years! Yet they forgot to revere him—they forgot his deeds and mighty wonders. As they lost sight of his goodness, God's chosen people gave in to various

---

34. Dawn Marie Wilson, Facebook, September 3, 2019, accessed April 2, 2025, https://tinyurl.com/s5hy3hxd.

destructive attitudes and behaviors, such as complaining, worrying, making comparisons, acting in unbelief, rebelling, and more. Lest we mock their forgetfulness, we might want to gain insight by asking the Holy Spirit, *Am I remembering the goodness of God?*

While we may forget God's goodness, in his goodness, he never forgets us!

The blessed truth is that while we may forget God's goodness, in his goodness, he never forgets us! He is faithful to hear our repentant cries. In our struggles, we might think that God somehow stopped listening to us, but throughout Scripture, he is revealed as the God who hears, sees, and knows us—and out of his goodness and faithfulness, he chooses to remember us.

Growing in Goodness

Our heavenly Father surrounds us with his goodness. God *was good* to us in sending Jesus to be our Savior, and before we were even born, he ordained good works for us to accomplish.[35] He *is good* now, making us more like Jesus by transforming us through the Holy Spirit. And he *will be good* as he fulfills his plan to banish evil forever in eternity. Remembering such bountiful goodness can cause us to express gratitude and worship him.

Consider some ways God expresses his goodness. Nahum said God is our hiding place. Some translations use the words *refuge, haven, stronghold,* or *fortress*. In modern culture, we tend to use the phrase *a safe place*. Knowing God as our safe place encourages us to trust him freely and fully. He is our place of bona fide security because we'll

---

35. Ephesians 2:10

never be in a circumstance outside of his control. Our good Father is our sturdy shelter when life assaults us, whether with poor health, a relationship struggle, financial stress, or any other difficulties. He recognizes and welcomes those who seek his aid, no matter how desperate the struggle.

We also remember God's goodness after he provides for us, especially when his supply is unusual or miraculous. I'll never forget praying over my last few dollars while serving with a traveling revival team. But then God used an elderly woman to provide an overflowing gift basket of necessities. I thanked her profusely, of course, but my gratitude overflowed as I prayed, "Oh, Lord, you are *so good* to me."

Knowing God as our safe place encourages us to trust him freely and fully.

Every good gift comes from our Father. He showers us with his goodness by forgiving our sins, changing our sinful hearts, granting us peace, strengthening us to fight temptation, providing life purpose, and so much more. The greatest gift he's given us—besides his precious Son—is the Bible.

Conduits of Goodness

When we remember how God has blessed us, we become better conduits of his goodness. We don't want to keep it to ourselves. We want the world to know him. We want others to experience his forgiveness, love, provision, protection, and guidance. Such concern that people know God's goodness goes beyond worldly humanitarianism. It expresses the very heart of God for the world. Because goodness is part of the fruit of the Holy Spirit—fruit he cultivates and harvests in our lives—the Spirit shows us how to encourage others.

Believers can exhibit godly goodness, goodness that is humble and authentic, through many practical means. The most obvious way to exhibit goodness—acts of service—might include running errands, volunteering at shelters, or assisting with tasks. We display goodness in our generosity, whether through donations, gifts, or even buying groceries or paying a bill for someone.

We express goodness in our relationships through active listening, seeking to understand others' hurts, showing compassion, working to resolve conflicts, treating people with dignity, and relating to them with grace and forgiveness. Goodness shares encouraging words to uplift people, and it's especially effective when accompanied by Scripture. Goodness isn't merely good works, though. Those works stem from the soul's goodness, which is sourced by the Spirit.

God delights in our goodness as we pray and intercede for others in their struggles. They may never know, but he sees!

Dear Father God, I know that, at its root, doing good is not about me. It's about honoring you as I reflect your goodness. It's about pouring your love on those in need. I want to be a light in the darkness, to share your goodness in the world. Thank you for allowing me to do this with your wisdom and as the Holy Spirit empowers me to see and meet needs. May your goodness continue to follow me all the days of my life because of Jesus in me.

I Know God Is Good

by Carolyn Gaston

I will not hate my heartache.
I know he holds my tears in his hand.
I will not fret in my fear.
I know his love is greater.
I will not complain in the chaos.
I know he's in control.

I may not feel God's goodness in this
    moment, in my heartache,
In my fear, in the chaos. But I know God is good.

I will not be bitter in the battle.
I know he's fighting for me.
I will not be discouraged in the darkness.
I know he is my light.
I will not be frustrated in the fire.
I know he'll bring me through.

I may not see God's goodness in this moment, in the battle,
In the darkness, in the fire. But I know God is good.

I will not wallow in my weakness.
I know he is my strength.
I will not sulk in my sadness.
I know he is my joy.
I will not despair in my depression.
I know he'll lift me up.

I may not find God's goodness in this
    moment, in my weakness,
In my sadness, in my depression. But I know God is good.

I will not worry in the wilderness.
I know he'll make a way.
I will not crumble in the confusion.
I know he is my peace.
I will not despise my dilemma.
I know he has a plan.

I may not taste God's goodness in this
    moment, in the wilderness,
In the confusion, in my dilemma. But I know God is good.

Lord, in this world filled with pain and problems, suffering and sorrow, help me be still and know you are God and know you are good. Even when I can't feel, see, find, or taste your goodness, help me believe you are working all things together for good for those who love you and are called according to your purpose.[36] Lord, I really want to feel your goodness as I sense your holy presence. I want to see your goodness as you reveal your faithfulness. I want to find your goodness in the blessings I take for granted. I want to taste your goodness as I learn to savor your gentleness. Father, I believe your goodness will follow me all the days of my life.[37]

---

36. Romans 8:28
37. Psalm 23:6

Goodness Rocks

by Pattie Reitz

MIDDLE AGE IS such a weird time of life. Some women lose their filter and say, "No one cares. I can do whatever I want." Others decide now is a great time to impart wisdom randomly with impunity. It's no wonder the middle years are called the "sandwich" years. We look back on our decades of life one minute, and we're planning for our future the next. We're often caring for children or grandchildren and aging parents at the same time. Sometimes our own health turns, and we find ourselves caring for ourselves or our spouse. The past and the future smoosh into our present, and we may feel overwhelmed or forgotten by God.

Can you relate? I sure can.

I'm not one who doesn't care—if anything, I care too much. I have wrestled with this often, and I've decided that this is who I am: a woman who loves her family and the world, who wants to serve God, and who is constantly amazed at the goodness of God. I want to sing it at the top of my lungs! He has been faithful in so many ways. When I stop to think about it, I'm overcome with gratitude. My guess is that you feel the same when you look back on your life.

GATHER THE GOODNESS

One thing that helps when I feel forgotten or overwhelmed in the chaos of life is expressing gratitude directly to the Lord. Acknowledging and thanking God for his goodness and all his blessings is a wonderful exercise for us when we're overwhelmed.

No matter what challenges come our way in this life, God's goodness is everywhere.

I was reminded anew of this truth recently as our praise team sang "Goodness of God" at our worship service. With tears welling in my eyes and love pumping through my heart, I felt God's goodness in a new and comforting way. No matter what challenges come our way in this life, God's goodness is everywhere.

Ebenezers

Many times in the Bible, God's people built a cairn, a pile of stones, to mark and remember God's provision, blessing, and love. In one place, Samuel set one large stone and named it Ebenezer—"stone of help."[38] When I consider God's goodness, I think of three *Ebenezers* in my life: protection from injury, comfort in emotional hurt, and preservation of my hearing.

Protection from Harm

I wouldn't wish the misfortune of a car accident on anyone, but I've sadly been in several. One in particular stands out to me as an example of the goodness of God in action.

I was driving back to my college dorm from visiting my high school best friend one January weekend when snow began to fall. I slowed my speed to be safe, but I hit a slick spot and slid off the highway

---

38. Genesis 31; 1 Samuel 7

into a ditch. I was between Missouri towns, so I sat in my stalled car in the snow, praying for help. Within a few minutes, a station wagon pulled over, and the man asked if he could take me to the next town to call a tow truck.

I gratefully agreed when I saw his wife waving in the passenger seat. They drove me to the nearest house, where I used my calling card to make two important calls—to roadside assistance and my father. Dad told me to get a hotel room near where my car had been towed, and he'd take care of the bill. I also made a call to my college dorm office to let them know why I would miss our meeting that night.

The tow truck driver took my car to a car repair shop, and he pointed me toward a nearby hotel. I walked into the lobby with my duffel bag, and the desk clerk said, "Just a moment," into the phone and asked me, "Hi, are you Pattie?"

I was flabbergasted but nodded *yes*.

She held the phone for me. "This call is for you."

"Hello?" I asked. A friendly woman's voice told me that my friend at the dorm office, who was her future daughter-in-law, had called her. My friend told her about my accident and asked her to check to make sure I was okay. She invited me to stay with them instead of paying for a hotel room.

Only God could have orchestrated my accident outside the town where several of my college friends had connections. Only God could have provided a station wagon with a friendly (and safe) young family inside to drive me to a nearby house where someone allowed me to use their phone to call for help. And only God could have protected me from injury on a snowy road.

Friendship Breakup

Years later, as a young pastor's wife with children, I experienced a devastating friendship breakup at church. The friends I thought I had were not mine—when one decided to reject me, the others followed suit. For many months, I was in a lonely place. Never had I needed Jesus to be my friend more. He was faithful. He comforted my heart with the peace of his Spirit, and he provided several other friends in town and at work in moments I needed them.

Never had I needed Jesus to be my friend more.

I will never forget the goodness of Jesus during that time, to me and to our family. Within a year, we found ourselves in a new town and church, forging new friendships and connections that lasted for many years to come.

Ear Surgery Miracle

During the year we lived in South Texas, I had a recurring ear infection. I repeatedly went to the doctor, got an antibiotic for the infection, and felt better after the ten-day treatment. Then a week or two later, the ear pain returned. This went on for months until I received a referral to a specialist. Just before we were set to move to Alaska, the doctors diagnosed me with a condition called cholesteatoma. Six months later, I had surgery to remove the growth and rebuild my right ear drum.

It wasn't until afterward that I realized how serious this condition was. Left untreated, I might have lost my life instead of just my hearing. As it was, I had two follow-up surgeries. One was successful in repairing damage. The other—not successful in fixing my hearing loss. Eventually, I qualified for and received a hearing aid, which has greatly improved my quality of life.

Goodness Rocks!

God is so good! He provided me the "stones" of protection during and after an accident, healing in my heart after losing my friends, and of course, saving my life and my hearing. I don't often talk about it, but if it wasn't for God's goodness and care for me, I might not be here today to tell you about what a good God he is.

If it wasn't for God's goodness and care for me, I might not be here today to tell you about what a good God he is.

If there is an advantage of being in middle age, this is it. I can remember the goodness of God in the past, see it every day, and know that in the future, no matter what happens, God will still be adding to my pile of memory stones.

Savoring God's Goodness

by Charlaine Martin

*Oh, taste and see that the LORD is good;
Blessed is the man who trusts in Him!*

PSALM 34:8 (NKJV)

ONE EVENING, MY husband and I walked briskly around our local town square for exercise. I hadn't eaten dinner yet, and hunger pangs gnawed at me. *I'll get a snack on the way home,* I reasoned. As I pushed through our last round of the walk, steak, shrimp, and other tempting aromas enticed me from nearby eateries. Diners joyfully chatted inside and outside restaurants, savoring their tasty meals. *I want what they have so badly.*

"Honey, I'm starved. Can we get something to eat on the way home?" I asked.

"How about pizza?" he offered.

"Sounds great!" So, we headed to our favorite pizza shop. It smelled delicious, making my mouth water, and we eagerly placed our order. After it was served, we enjoyed our delectable, nourishing pizza. It was so much better than sniffing other people's meals or getting by on a snack.

Observing Christians savoring Scripture, being nourished in a healthy church, and enjoying fellowship with other believers is like watching someone eat an amazing meal with our noses pressed to the window—while starving. I'd experienced this as a teen. I joined the church a while after my boyfriend invited me to visit his, but I hadn't accepted Jesus as my Savior. I could see Christians relishing God's goodness as they dined on God's Word, basked in fellowship together, and lived the life I wanted so badly for myself. It wasn't until I was twenty-six that I experienced this new life. One morning, God showed me what was missing. So, I confessed my sin and prayed the prayer I'd often heard from our pastor's altar calls. My life dramatically changed. I could finally enjoy God's goodness for myself.

God's goodness comes to those who trust in Jesus as Savior.

In Psalm 34, David reflects on the time he ran from King Saul. He had received showbread—holy bread from God's altar—from the priest Ahimelech for himself and his men and received Goliath's sword for protection.[39] God provided for their needs. Then, David thought he could hide in Gath, but Gath's king didn't want him there. So, David—afraid for his life—pretended to be crazy.

This backdrop helps us get an insider's view of Psalm 34. We see how David cried out to God and how God delivered him from harm. [40] Later, he shares how God spared a man when he called on God to

---

39. 1 Samuel 21
40. Psalm 34:4

save him and sent angels to encamp around his men for protection.[41] In our passage, David invites us to experience God's goodness like he did, encouraging us to taste and see that the Lord is good.

Do you gaze inside, longing for what Christ's followers have? I invite you to accept Jesus as *your* Savior and ask him to guide you. Dine on the nourishment of God's Word. Drink in the pastor's sermons and Bible studies. Relish in the fellowship of other believers in a healthy, Bible-teaching church. Commune with God privately through daily Bible reading and prayer. Experience God's goodness for yourself, and your life will never be the same. God's goodness comes to those who trust in Jesus as Savior.

> *Lord, I don't want to sniff others' faith only to sample it. I want to savor your goodness. I want to drink the living water and never thirst[42]and take in the bread of life that I may never hunger.[43] I want to experience you every day. Thank you for loving me with your perfect love.*

---

41. Psalm 34:6–7
42. John 4:14
43. John 6:35

For the Kingdom of God is not a matter of what we eat or drink, but of living a life of goodness and peace and joy in the Holy Spirit. If you serve Christ with this attitude, you will please God, and others will approve of you, too.

Romans 14:17–18 (NLT)

Lift from Below

by Robin Steinweg

Put on then, as God's chosen ones, holy and beloved, compassionate hearts, kindness, humility, meekness, and patience . . . And above all these put on love, which binds everything together in perfect harmony.

COLOSSIANS 3:12, 14 (ESV)

"BE GOOD." WE'VE all heard this, but what in the world does it mean? Good at what? How do I become *good*?

I've looked up Bible verses on goodness and found "No one is good except God alone."[44] I can believe that! But since God tells us to bear this fruit of the Spirit and to clothe ourselves with qualities that encompass goodness, it must be possible for us too.

Right, Lord. You placed in me a desire to be good. Help me with it, please.

---

44. Mark 10:18 (ESV)

GATHER THE GOODNESS

Some years ago, an accident caused injury to my back. Over time, the pain increased. My doctor recommended physical therapy. One of the first things my therapist did was to train me to properly lift items so I wouldn't do further injury.

I practiced this for weeks before I realized it mirrored Christlike behavior. I had long prayed to have more of a servant's heart—to be more like Jesus. I wanted insight into how to lift and support others without coming off like I was superior or condescending. This was an unexpected way for the Lord to answer.

I had long prayed to have more of a servant's heart—to be more like Jesus.

Whether my goal is to lift an object or to lift another's burden, I can follow these guidelines:

- Be mindful and careful. Remember the therapist's training.
- Be mindful and prayerful. Remember my Master's words—I must choose to put on compassion, kindness, humility, gentleness, and patience: goodness.

- Crouch low. I'm likely to be injured if I try to lift from above.
- Bend low. Begin from a humble stance, not from any high or self-righteous mindset. I'll be less likely to wound someone's spirit.

- Get as close as possible to the object. Move obstacles out of the way in order to get closer.
- Get as close as possible to the person. Ask Jesus to give me his love for them and remove any obstacles in my attitude.

- Hold the object close to my core. I learned that an object held at arm's length weighs the equivalent of ten times more!
- Hold the person close to my heart. When God's goodness is my desire and he leads, the other's burden will seem light.

- Engage my core muscles.
- Engage my prayer muscles.

- Overcome the injury. Employ therapy techniques from an expert.
- Overcome evil with good. Rely on God's presence and goodness.

- Lift carefully, using the stronger muscles in my core and legs.
- Lift with loving care—not in my own strength, but with God's infinite strength and presence.

GATHER THE GOODNESS

Every time I crouch to safely lift an object, I'm reminded to lift another's burden from the humble heart of a servant. And to hold them close in prayer and in Jesus's selfless, infinite love. His is the goodness I desire.

---

*Every time I crouch to safely lift an object,
I'm reminded to lift another's burden
from the humble heart of a servant.*

The prayer of my heart is to put on Christ. Only he can help me lift others from below—from a loving posture—with his goodness.

How Do You Hide a Mountain?

by Janice Metot

*I would have lost heart unless I had believed
That I would see the goodness of the LORD
In the land of the living.*

PSALM 27:13 (NKJV)

IT WAS MY first visit to Washington State. The mountain view from the plane overwhelmed me—there was nothing like this back east. On the drive to my uncle's house, the range towered over me, extending for miles, otherworldly. Although a trip to Mt. Rainier was part of our plans, I could not wait. I barely said hello and asked him for a good place to take pictures. Amused, he gave me directions but added, "Don't be disappointed. You can only see the mountain if it is out."

I brushed off his words and scoffed, "How do you hide a mountain?"

GATHER THE GOODNESS

The Day the Fog Rolled In

Mountains offer a breathtaking perspective, but I have always liked being in high places where I could see the big picture. While growing up, my retreat was a beautiful oval-shaped maple tree. It stood tall and straight, a sentinel at the pinnacle of my world. I watched over the flats that spread out almost a mile, with its golden grass shimmering in the summer breeze.

I have always liked being in high places where I could see the big picture.

It was the year I was in fourth grade. I perched on the "chair" formed from its rough limbs. I took in the earthy smell of its bark. A gentle breeze washed over me, bringing the invigorating aroma of freshly mowed hay. I leaned back, eyes closed as I sank into the tree, unleashing a fresh flow of tears. The day had been a disaster. Hurt and angry thoughts buzzed through my mind, unfocused, not unlike those pesky little black flies that swirled around my head in early spring.

"Help me up!" A clamoring voice broke through my racing thoughts and brought me back to the present. There was my sister, trying to jump up to the lowest branch. Reluctantly, I braced myself and reached down to hoist her up. "How long are you going to stay up here?" she demanded.

"I'm never coming down!"

☙

I was *smitten, crazy,* and *obsessed* with David, a boy in my class. I dreaded square dancing in the gym, as my palms sweated profusely whenever I grabbed his hand. When I tried to speak to him, if my words came out, they were clumsy and fell to the floor. Diana, my best friend since first grade, liked him too, and it made me jealous to see them easily talking and laughing together.

Desperate, I had written a love letter, agonizing over every word. Then, with a splash of perfume and a sheer force of will, I declared it done. I had just enough time to privately leave it on his desk first thing in the morning, but as I sat down, instant regret left me paralyzed. I imagined quickly jumping out of my desk to rescue my dignity, but it was too late. Diana and David entered the room together and took their seats. For the rest of the day, I could not bear to look at either of them and tried to look busy. At some point, I saw him find the letter, read it, and stare at me.

For two horrible days, there had been no response. Diana came into school on the third day and handed me a letter from him. I just said, "Oh, thanks," and nonchalantly stuck it in my desk.

On my way home, I pulled out the letter and carefully opened it. I gasped as I read his words, "I don't like you. You're as ugly as . . ." Slowly, I ripped the letter to pieces as I got off the bus, never looking back as they fluttered away in the wind.

When the Son Broke Through

It was too hot to play outside that summer, and we were tired of our games. A neighbor invited us to his church for Vacation Bible School (VBS), and our parents urged us along because it would be "good for us." With the rest of our neighborhood friends, off we went. To my surprise, it was a good week. I liked hearing the stories about Jesus. My heart was riveted as the invitation came to accept Jesus as my Savior, and I went straight to the altar without hesitation.

I was very happy to know that God loved me, although when VBS was over, life at home and in school was the same. I still struggled and did not feel any different. Yet inside, something major had changed.

GATHER THE GOODNESS

Navigating the Storms

As the years went on, my social life continued to plummet. I seemed caught in a pattern that played over and over, like a song on repeat. The hurt and disappointments piled up, and I lost sight of my value and future. I withdrew and read—a lot—to cope with the ever-increasing stresses of school and home. My parents never knew how much I struggled or how bad I felt. I kept it all inside. I continued to watch over my brothers and sisters, a role I played well, and it kept me hidden. I learned to go through the motions and stay invisible, but the pressure in my heart grew unbearable.

Beginning at a young age, I discovered that journaling helped me pour it all out. To my amazement, once I got past the raw emotion of hating my life, other words began to flow. They were like a parent's voice moving through my pen, providing encouragement, direction, and wisdom. The words calmed my soul and gave me strength.

Although dark thoughts continued to plague me, little by little, as I pressed on, I found goodness in life. No matter the struggle, every morning was a reset that caused supernatural joy to start my day. Like Dorothy in *The Wizard of Oz*, my world went from black and white to full living color as the beauty of creation, the excitement of motherhood, and learning to rest in God's presence opened my soul to embrace the many good things God was bringing into my life.

God's presence dissolves the storm and lifts the fog in our hearts, bringing clarity and joy during many sorrows.

Many years later when I pored through my old journals, I realized it was God's voice that had guided me all along. He heard that little girl's prayer and came to her rescue. I didn't always understand or cooperate, but with the Spirit of God living in my heart, I knew I would never be alone.

A Mountain Cannot Stay Hidden

My uncle taught me that heavy cloud cover, mist, or fog reduces visibility and makes it impossible to see the mountain. Those who were not aware could easily pass by and never know what lay behind the veil. It took a clear day for the mountain to make its stunning appearance.

Similarly, when the trials of life destroy our hope, many of us miss God's goodness. It is natural to harden our hearts, even to the point of doubting God exists. Unless we receive him, his manifest beauty and majesty are hidden behind the veil.

God's presence dissolves the storm and lifts the fog in our hearts, bringing clarity and joy during many sorrows. God is good. All the time. No matter the situation or the weather.

Good Gracious!

by Kathy Carlton Willis

The little girl perched on the porch swing,
Talked with God.
She soaked in his presence beside her
And in her.

The young girl learned of God's goodness,
Walked with God.
She held up a mirror to reflect his love
Inside her.

The teen girl forgot her childlike faith,
Identity lost.
She stumbled and struggled and strayed,
Misplaced peace.

The church girl worked for God's approval,
Brainwashed faith.
She feared their threats, despising the shame,
Heart trembled.

The career girl chased her dreams and goals,
Self-driven.
She found her heart wounded and weary,
Lost her way.

The little girl's Father visited her.
All grown up.
She had lost touch of his goodness,
His kind love.

The daughter of God recalled his heart
So gentle.
She yearned for the faith of a young child,
For goodness.

The woman connected to the Vine,
Sap of God.
She welcomed the glow of his goodness,
Found her way.

The believer unearthed God's treasure,
Trusting still.
She longed to feel and understand him more
And live it.

The faithful woman served her Lord
Because of love.
She noticed the neglected ones' needs,
Empathy born.

The disciple experienced God's virtues
Flowing through her
As she abided in him again,
Remembered.

The little girl perched on the porch swing,
Talked with God.
She soaked in his presence beside her
And in her.

When Goodness Takes the Helm

by Joni Topper

"YES, BUT ARE you any good at it?" It's a simple way to start a conversation. When a new student tells my husband they are a ball player or piano player or whatever, he often responds with that question. My husband is a seventy-three-year-old introvert, and his comfort level with elementary school-aged children is limited. Still, he works with kids at church on Wednesday nights.

Sometimes striking up a conversation with a new kid is easy. Sometimes it's not. He gets acquainted with students as they reveal their accomplishments. When I see him do this, I know he's being intentional. He works through his own shyness to build a connection because he knows he cannot be a successful teacher without connection.

Why would he do that? Why do any of us push through our personal discomfort? Does God expect us to perform, to be good?

Understand

Various good fruit or qualities of the Holy Spirit are described in Scripture. "But the fruit of the Spirit is love, joy, peace, patience, kindness, goodness, faithfulness, gentleness, self-control; against such things there is no law."[45] *Karpos,* the Greek word for fruit, describes what is naturally produced by a living organism.[46] When we become a Christian, the Holy Spirit is that living organism in us. Consequently, the qualities described in this verse are produced naturally. The Holy Spirit produces fruit that shoves our sinful nature aside. The internal tug-of-war we all have begins to make room for the light that is Christ living in us. So, you see, goodness is a consequence of the presence of the Holy Spirit. It's as natural as breathing.

The internal tug-of-war we all have begins to make room for the light that is Christ living in us.

When I breathe air into a balloon and then release it, air rushes out. If the same balloon is filled with water, what will pour out when released? Of course, water will pour out. The same principle is true when we invite the Holy Spirit to live in us. His characteristics, or fruit, will flow from us naturally.

What does the word *goodness* mean to you? The Greek word *agathosune,* from *agathos,* describes virtue and excellence demonstrated in active kindness.[47] Goodness is shown in human form by a generous heart that cares for and obtains what is beneficial to others. Because goodness describes behavior that seeks the best for others rather than self, it's no surprise that the word is tied to God's presence.

---

45. Galatians 5: 22–23 (ESV)
46. Walter A. Elwell, *Baker's Evangelical Dictionary of Biblical Theology,* "entry for 'Fruit'" (Grand Rapids: Baker Book House Company, 1996), 614–16, as included in Bible Study Tools (website), accessed March 5, 2025, https://www.biblestudytools.com/dictionary/fruit.
47. *Strong's Lexicon,* "Agathosune: Goodness," Bible Hub (website), accessed March 5, 2025, https://biblehub.com/greek/19.htm.

Jesus used these words to describe himself, "I am the good shepherd."[48] He could have called himself the perfect shepherd, the protective shepherd, or the ever-present shepherd. However, in using just the word *good*, he covered every important attribute of a shepherd and summed them up in one word. Good. Goodness came from Jesus because it was his very essence. It's a universal virtue that everyone appreciates. Now, let's dive into how this goodness grows within us.

Facilitate

Growing in our faith can seem daunting. That's because we forget that the strength we need comes from the Lord. We don't have to muster strength on our own. Peter knew this when he wrote these words: "For this very reason, make every effort to supplement your faith with virtue."[49] Isn't faith enough? Well, yes, it is enough—but God has so much more to offer. He says we can actually produce fruit—*good* fruit. If you've ever had a fruit tree that didn't bear a crop, you will understand. It's so disappointing to know there's great potential for beauty and nourishment and reproduction. Fruit offers proof of life, proof of identity.

Fruit offers proof of life, proof of identity.

Peter said once you've established that you believe God—that you have faith—then add the fruit of the Spirit. It's as though he told us where to start and then how to proceed. Start with faith. Add goodness (virtue). Then add knowledge. Then add self-control, etc.[50] Peter was

---

48. John 10:11 (NKJV)
49. 2 Peter 1:5 (ESV)
50. 2 Peter 1:5–7 (ESV)

not giving a to-do list but telling what faith will look like as it grows in us. He painted a picture of a beautiful believer. This is what you will look like as you grow in Christ.

I want to look like Christ. How about you?

The first words of that verse, "for this very reason," piqued my curiosity. Did it yours? I wanted to know what he meant. For *what* reason? "His divine power has granted to us all things that pertain to life and godliness, through the knowledge of him who called us to his own glory and excellence."[51] This Scripture gives us a roadmap and, at the same time, says, don't worry; God will help you in this endeavor. He's packed your bags for this journey with everything you need.

Take It Personally

Embrace the concept. Becoming a new creation in Christ will change you. It will allow Christ to be formed in you. Ask yourself some questions.

- Where have I seen goodness that I knew came from God?

- Have I ever associated someone's good work with their relationship to God? Why?

- What fruit of the Spirit seems the most difficult for me to personify? (See Galatians 5:22–23.)

- The above Scripture says his divine power has granted all things that pertain to life and godliness. What are some of the resources he's given to me that will allow me to live a godly life? Am I utilizing those resources?

---

51. 2 Peter 1:3 (ESV)

- Am I ready to accept the changes in myself that happen when I allow the Holy Spirit to produce fruit in me?

Apply

While going through her child's piano workbook, my sister noticed that several pages were skipped. Upon closer inspection, she realized that the songs the teacher skipped were all hymns.

Apparently, the teacher had deliberately skipped those songs because of their connection with faith. My sister felt it was important to discuss it with her child. I'll never forget what she told her daughter. "We are going to go back and pick up these songs the teacher asked you to skip. I want you to play each of them as though you were playing them for the Lord."

Her explanation of *how* she hoped her child would play the songs was tied to the spirit of worship she hoped to hear as the notes rang out. She wanted those songs, in particular, to be played as a reflection of her heart before the Lord—to reflect the goodness of God.

The more we allow him to dwell in us, the more natural it is for his goodness to impact those around us.

In the same manner, our lives of faith reflect the resources we draw upon. Acceptance of the divine power present in us through the Holy Spirit gives us everything we need. When we let Christ live in us, the world around us will see his goodness. Christlike goodness will pour out of us like water poured from the balloon. People will be touched by our natural inclination to seek the welfare of others.

GATHER THE GOODNESS

Goodness is something we offer each other, but more importantly, it indicates our relationship with God. In the presence of goodness, we recognize one of God's characteristics. The more we allow him to dwell in us, the more natural it is for his goodness to impact those around us. God's goodness at work in and through us. It is very good.

Faithfulness

He Rescues Me

by Denise Margaret Ackerman

The one who doubts is like a billowing surge of the sea that is blown about and tossed by the wind.

JAMES 1:6 (AMP)

When pressures mount, and skies are gray,
I turn my eyes to seek your face.
You send relief; my fears are eased.
Your grace and mercy rescue me.

Each anxious thought and worldly care,
I lift them up for you to bear.
Thank you, Lord, my faithful friend.
I'll love and thank you 'til the end.

When storms arise, and waves crash in,
I tune my ears above the din.
Your word brings peace; it calms the sea.
Your grace and mercy rescue me.

Each anxious thought and worldly care,
I lift them up for you to bear.
Thank you, Lord, my faithful friend.
I'll love and trust you 'til the end.

I rest in you, my faithful Lord.
I know you're near throughout life's storms.
I'll trust in you; where'er I go.
All doubts will flee when you are known.

Each anxious thought and worldly care,
I lift them up for you to bear.
Thank you, Lord, my closest friend.
I'll love and serve you 'til the end.

Oh, Father, you are the anchor I can rely on throughout the storms I face in this life. I praise and thank you for your faithfulness in caring for your children. Help me to trust in your loving-kindness, even when my feelings are being tossed by the stormy trials I'm facing.

RV There, God?

by Kolleen Lucariello

For years, we'd entertained the idea of owning an RV once Pat retired so we could travel across the country. It became common when we saw one—whether a camper being towed behind their vehicle or a motorhome cruising along—to imagine the adventures we could have with one of our own. We'd had countless conversations debating the right size and the ideal model—should we tow it or drive it?

When I spotted the small RV parked outside a local dealership, my curiosity was piqued. So, I suggested we stop and check it out. We'd never know unless we explored our options, would we? We didn't stop that night, but a few days later, we were parked next to it.

The Sales Pitch We Couldn't Resist

The salesman didn't just open the door to the RV; he painted a picture of a retirement filled with adventure, freedom, and endless possibilities. The RV in the parking lot had already been spoken for, but they found a similar one at a dealership a few hours away. With the salesman's assurance that we were joining a company faithfully committed to its customers—and his insistence that we'd regret walking away—we signed on the dotted line. Just like that, we now owned a retirement home on wheels.

We returned to pick up our new home-on-the-go just days later. With excitement oozing out of us, we planned our maiden voyage. Our first stop? My parents! They lived a few hours away and had owned several motorhomes, so we knew they'd have plenty of tips to share with us. About a week later, we were packed and ready to roll. I didn't think we would ever stop smiling.

We had barely driven three hundred yards from our driveway when the check engine light came on. Pat pulled over, and we started flipping through the owner's manual, hoping to find an answer. Realizing our effort was unsuccessful, we decided to drive it back to the dealership for help.

"I'm sorry, but no one in the service department is available. Here's a phone number you can call."

After a conversation with the tech, a guarantee it was nothing more than an error code and completely safe to drive, we took off for our first adventure.

The Unreliable Sales Pitch

What we didn't realize at the time was how quickly the reassurances from the salesman, who promised we could always rely on them, would fade. The promises that they'd always be there to help with any questions, repairs, or support we needed were soon broken. As time passed, we understood the difference between a sales pitch and true commitment. The real test came after our cross-country adventure to California for a wedding.

We made our way out west, traveling along Route 66, with our Mother Road Passport book guiding us to each new destination. One by one, we explored attractions and reveled in the beauty of scenic

America. And one by one, we added to our list of broken RV items. We'd been warned that with all the shifting while driving, things were bound to break. But when the hot water tank blew in Arizona, and a stop at a dealership for help produced none, it took an immense amount of self-control for me not to blow up too.

A Journey of Adjustments

Mile after mile, we adjusted to the conditions of one thing after another breaking in the RV. With each new issue, we had to adjust—slow down, recalibrate our expectations, and realize that the adventure wasn't just about the destinations but how we responded to the unexpected.

The adventure wasn't just about the destinations but how we responded to the unexpected.

This became increasingly difficult as the growing list of repairs revealed the dealership's lack of faithfulness. They had once promised unwavering support, but now, when we needed them most, that promise was nowhere to be found. Calls went unanswered, service appointments stretched for months, and after assuring us that all work had been completed, our next outing exposed their failure to winterize the RV—leading to a burst water line. The very ones who had promised to stand by us had become unreliable, and the lingering uncertainty made us hesitant to fully embrace the freedom the RV was supposed to offer.

RV There, God?

Without even realizing it, I can treat God the same way. I've been hesitant to step out in faith, afraid that if things go wrong, I'll be left stranded. Has that happened to you? We want to trust his promises, but past disappointments make us cautious. Yet, unlike the dealership, we can be assured that God's faithfulness isn't a marketing strategy—it's his very nature. "God is not a man, so he does not lie. He is not human, so he does not change his mind. Has he ever spoken and failed to act? Has he ever promised and not carried it through?"[52]

When he says he will guide, provide, and sustain us, we can believe him. The question is: Will we let fear hold us back, or will we trust that God will always come through? He has never failed before, and he won't start now.

His promises are not based on convenience or availability—they are part of his very character. He doesn't forget, delay, or disappear when things get tough. Scripture tells us that even "if we are unfaithful, he remains faithful, for he cannot deny who he is."[53] Unlike human promises that can fall short, God's faithfulness is unwavering, enduring, and always present. When he says he will never leave us or forsake us, he means it.[54] What a gift to know that we serve a God who stands by his Word—not because he has to, but because it's who he is!

While road trips come with detours, his faithfulness never does.

A friend of ours has since repaired the RV, but our trust in the dealership? Well, that remains a bit broken. And yet, that's okay—because I've learned to put my trust in the One who never fails. The one who always answers when I ask, "RV there, God?" And without fail, his answer has always been—absolutely! Every mile, every mishap, every moment, he will be there, proving once again that while road trips come with detours, his faithfulness never does.

---

52. Numbers 23:19 (NLT)
53. 2 Timothy 2:13 (NLT)
54. Hebrews 13:5

Faith in Sioux Falls

by Hally J. Wells

THE NURSE APPEARED puzzled as she washed my mother's feet. Mom's overdue bed bath became a concern when Nurse Kelly's warm, gentle touch resulted in a bizarre shedding. Big crumbs, followed by strips of skin, fell from Mom's left foot, each purging wipe rendering more dead, dirty, and perhaps diseased skin. Was this yet another medical mystery to be figured out?

The Crisis

My mother and stepfather, on their return trip to their Elsberry, Missouri, home, found themselves in a Sioux Falls, South Dakota, emergency room. My seventy-five-year-old mother, Melba, my stepfather, Ben, and another couple had spent a leisurely week trail riding and camping in their respective travel trailers. They'd enjoyed equine exercise, beautiful early-fall vistas in the Black Hills, camaraderie with dear friends, and pleasing weather. But their trip turned life-threatening when Mom felt "weird" and winded when they stopped for lunch.

Having parked their trucks and trailers a distance from the restaurant, Mom struggled to keep up with the group as they trekked across the parking lot. Although she was aware of an odd feeling, they ate lunch and drove further south to Northern Nebraska and a campground where they'd unload the horses and spend their final night.

Ben had begun unloading their Fox Trotters, Paco and Hershey, when Mom said she thought she should get checked out. He finished putting the two in their stalls and took Mom to the nearest urgent care facility in Vermillion, South Dakota—a short distance back across the Nebraska state line. Once at urgent care, the doctor suggested they admit Mom into the hospital across the street for observation. So, Ben went back to camp to finish his tasks and would return for Mom in the morning. Surely, she'd just caught a little bug or virus, and she'd be better after a night of antibiotics and fluids. My stepfather had no idea what a tenuous situation Mom was in.

When Ben arrived at the Vermillion hospital the next morning, he was told his wife had been transferred to a much larger hospital an hour away in Sioux Falls. Since there was no phone service at the campsite, he had no way of knowing Mom had been moved overnight. He drove immediately to Sioux Falls. Once there, time morphed. Did it slow down or speed up? Or was it a bit of both?

My mom had an emergency tracheotomy and began the fight of her life.

Ben later said that mere minutes after arriving and locating Mom, it felt like he was watching her fade away. He left her side to find the on-duty doctor, and when the physician returned to the room, he called a code blue. My mom had an emergency tracheotomy and began the fight of her life.

Medical Mystery

Twenty-four hours passed between Mom's first symptoms and the call I received the next day. I was on the job I'd started only weeks earlier when the phone rang. Ben shared what had happened, and by that night, my sister, Ellen, and I were in Sioux Falls—an eight-hour drive from our home.

Over the next few days, several specialists examined my mother. She had quickly and mysteriously gone from an active, healthy, horse-riding senior to an incapacitated, weak old woman with a ventilator doing her breathing and a dire prognosis.

There seemed to be no reason for Mom's rapid decline. Theories were considered and discarded one after another. Had she been bitten by a disease-carrying tick and developed Lyme disease? Mom's body was examined head-to-toe for bites. There was a small mark on her belly, but that amounted to nothing more than a bruise—compliments of her saddle horn.

A ventilator was doing Mom's breathing, and with droopy eyelids and facial paralysis, non-functioning lungs, and heavy limbs, Mom was in critical condition. However, she retained her mental faculties and soon communicated a desire for paper and pen. She'd help the doctors help her. We purchased a clipboard and a ream of copy paper, and she wrote the answers to all the questions her family members and physicians asked. My mother has always had beautiful handwriting, and it was only mildly impacted by her devastating illness.

Neurologists, pulmonologists, immunologists, and epidemiologists worked to identify what ailment had stricken Mom. Food poisoning was ruled out. Diagnostic spinal taps were conducted, and a dangerously potent botulism antitoxin, flown in from Chicago and picked up by a hospital pharmacist, was administered. Ben, my siblings, mom's friends and extended family, and I were terrified! My mother was not.

GATHER THE GOODNESS

Faith Like Mount Rushmore

My mother spent thirty days in that Sioux Falls hospital. Her sisters, my sister and I, a niece, and Ben made trips there and back. I don't believe Mom was alone at any time during her lengthy stay. We slept in her room, in waiting rooms, and our cars, and, occasionally, in one of the city's hotel rooms. We wanted to be there to advocate and help communicate for her, and we wanted every moment God gave us with her.

We wanted every moment God gave us with her.

Not once did I observe my mother lose patience as she struggled to express herself, grappling with pen and paper. Not once did her good nature fade—even when we teased her about her bare rear peeking out of the bottom of the harness that nurses used to move Mom when she couldn't move herself. We were reminded of an oddly similar scene from *Dreamer* when veterinarians treat a lame horse named Soñador. That sounds very wrong, but sometimes, hurting hearts need humor.

She calmed our fears when she managed to write, sign, and point out an explanation for her one disintegrating foot. Mom had bathed her left foot's calloused heels and toes in a corrosive, overnight treatment just before falling ill. Fearing she'd fall if both feet were bagged in plastic, she'd done only one. So, after the most critical days had passed, the sponge bath revealed the restorative power of Mom's one-sided *pedicare*.

Mom was abundantly appreciative toward the wonderful nurses and doctors who cared for her, thankful to clergy who visited and prayed with her, blessed with prayers of loved ones nearby and at home in Missouri. She remained faithful to God. Just as she'd lived her life prior to that fateful day, my mother exhibited strength alongside grace. Though she fought strenuously to survive, she trusted God! Faithful throughout the entire ordeal, Mom wanted to live, but she did not fear death. She proclaimed she knew what waited for her.

Answers

When all the questions had been answered, doctors determined that Mom had contracted Miller Fisher syndrome, a form of Guillain-Barré syndrome. She did recover. In fact, she turned seventy-six a month after finally being released and returning home to Missouri. She breathed on her own, walked, and rode horses again. She also shared her story. Overwhelmed by the incredible healing power of her heavenly Father, Mom asked Ellen and me to tell her story, in her words, during a service at her church.

Answers found in the Bible provide assurances of what awaits all who trust in him.

    Medical professionals painstakingly tested theories and ruled out possibilities to determine what illness had assaulted Mom. With those answers, they treated and healed her.

    Faithful believers like my precious mother have studied God's Word and ways. Answers found in the Bible provide assurances of what awaits all who trust in him.

Never let loyalty and kindness leave you!
Tie them around your neck as a reminder.
Write them deep within your heart.

PROVERBS 3:3 (NLT)

Wellspring for Weariness

by Becki James

"If anyone thirsts, let him come to me and drink. Whoever believes in me, as the Scripture has said, 'Out of his heart will flow rivers of living water.'"

JOHN 7:37–38 (ESV)

SHE KNELT DOWN, scooped the dirt, and let it fall through her calloused fingers. The earth was dry, desperate for rain. Her face reddened with heat—perspiration beaded against the wide-brimmed hat. Lifting it, she wiped her forehead, smearing the grime into her pores. She squinted. The sun seemed to pulse through the sky, vaporizing life and energy. Thirst dried her throat. The stream had been waterless for weeks. She groaned as she knuckled her weight to stand. Shuffling to the rain barrel, she grasped the ladle and raised the lid. Bone-dry.

Have you ever felt like that? Exhausted by the conditions around you or at the mercy of some uncontrollable factor? I have. The past few years drove my stress thermometer to the red zone. A huge relocation set off a series of events that sapped my emotional strength. Loneliness deepened the fatigue, and I mourned the life I'd left behind.

Then, a new storm devastated my world. While caring for a family member, I discovered a network of deception, beginning with the theft of my credit information. Sadness filled my heart. His treacheries unfolded, adding betrayal like the tyranny of an unrelenting drought. I sought solace in God, but the sorrow remained.

God's faithful presence is the wellspring for my weariness.

One morning, I sat staring outdoors. My mind drifted back to years gone by and a church I attended called River of Life. The name saturated my thoughts. I recalled a passage in Revelation where God described a river in heaven with the water of life flowing from his throne and of Jesus.[55] In that moment, healing began to flood over me, rushing from his heavenly sanctuary. I realized peace began at the source. God's faithful presence is the wellspring for my weariness.

When I asked Jesus to be my Lord and Savior, he promised to stay with me by sending his Spirit to dwell within me. John 7:37–39 says the Holy Spirit flows from me like rivers of living water. I had allowed my focus to fall on the number and duration of problems instead of drinking from the provision of God's character. Abundant life flows from the Father into me through Jesus and outward from me by the Spirit. He is the origin of my strength. The drought of my heart points me to the well of God's faithfulness.

Today, I sat absorbed in the beauty of a large picture on my wall. I stared at the sundrenched trees reflecting the constant nourishment

---

55. Revelation 22:1

of a gushing stream. I purchased it because the scene reminded me of romping through a similar creek with my younger brother. We swam in it. Fished in it. Played in it. And drank from its cool waters. That creek was the essence of our childhood.

But now, this image gives me fresh hope. Arid seasons will come—even linger. But God's presence flows dependably over my circumstances, hydrating me with his peace. He is the lifeblood of my existence. And that river—will never run dry.

Thank you, Father, for speaking through words, images, and nature. Thank you for allowing me to drink from the river of your faithfulness.

Fresh Each Day

by Denise Margaret Ackerman

Great is his faithfulness; his mercies begin afresh each morning.

LAMENTATIONS 3:23 (NLT)

I REALLY DIDN'T FEEL up to attending our ladies' event. A close family member was extremely discouraged, and I agonized about leaving their side. Due to my shaky emotions, I played out the scenario in my mind over again and again, praying that the Lord would give me discernment. Should I stay home and be available to my loved one, or should I participate in the church gathering? I was scheduled to share a personal testimony in front of the group and wasn't sure I could get through my talk without crying. Although my emotions weighed on me to stay home, I listened to the Lord's prompting and followed through on my commitment to attend.

Once I arrived at the gathering, it only took a few moments before the Lord assured me I was exactly where I needed to be. Sharon, our women's ministry leader, welcomed me with a loving hug and whispered, "We've been praying for you this morning."

My eyes filled with tears in response to her warm expression of concern, and at the same moment, the ache in my heart began to ease. The ladies had done a lovely job decorating the tables with pastel tablecloths adorned with appliqued flowers. The cheerful atmosphere helped me forget about the towering snowbanks lining our church parking lot and the mountain of concern I carried.

As guests and my fellow churchmates started to arrive, I focused on welcoming them. The more I paid attention to others, the less I felt weighed down by my burden. When Sharon opened our time together with prayer, I silently thanked the Lord I had trusted his leading.

After we enjoyed our homemade vegetable soup and salad, we were ushered into the church sanctuary, where Eleanor shared a devotion. Although a quiet, behind-the-scenes kind of lady, Eleanor's words were insightful, as she told us how making quilts reminds her about the Christian life. Before she begins a quilt, she pictures the design, the fabric and the steps required to create it. Once her project is underway, she often faces unexpected challenges that alter how her finished product looks. The end result is frequently different from what she had envisioned.

Eleanor went on to say that life can be that way. We have our ideas on how we think things should go and how the Lord will solve the many concerns we lift in prayer, but God does things differently than we expect.

My heart was moved and comforted by Eleanor's message. As I pondered the situation my loved one was experiencing and the hurt I felt over their suffering, I was reminded about the faithfulness of God. His love and care for us is beyond measure. His ways are not our ways, and his wisdom is beyond human comprehension. He knows what he is doing and exactly what needs to happen in each of our lives.

"He who began a good work in you will bring it to completion at the day of Jesus Christ."[56]

The Lord provided the strength I needed to tell others about the faithfulness and mercy he has demonstrated in my life.

When it came time for me to share my testimony, my outlook had been refreshed by the fellowship of other believers and the truths Eleanor shared from God's Word. Although I shed a few tears while talking, the Lord provided the strength I needed to tell others about the faithfulness and mercy he has demonstrated in my life.

Thank you, Lord, for the countless times you have refreshed my heavy heart. You are faithful. Please help me trust you as you complete your work in our lives.

---

56. Philippians 1:6 (ESV)

Now may the God of peace make you holy in every way, and may your whole spirit and soul and body be kept blameless until our Lord Jesus Christ comes again. God will make this happen, for he who calls you is faithful.

1 Thessalonians 5:23–24 (NLT)

God Cares for the Lost

by Denise Margaret Ackerman

THE GREAT JOY and healing I have received since surrendering my heart and life to the Lord has created a desire to see my loved ones experience those same blessings. It has been painful, and at times discouraging, to watch them suffer the consequences of their ungodly decisions. My heart has grieved as I stood with them during their difficulties. Still, I am compelled to keep my eyes on the faithfulness of God demonstrated in the Bible and to steadfastly pray for those who are living apart from him.

I am compelled to keep my eyes on the faithfulness of God.

Luke 15 is a wonderful chapter that displays God's heart of concern for the lost. Jesus shared three parables in response to the Pharisees' and scribes' negative mutterings regarding the way he accepted, welcomed, and even ate with sinners. These parables demonstrate the Lord's compassion for the lost as well as his celebration when they repent and turn back to seek his purpose for their lives.

I invite you to read Luke 15 and ask the Lord to encourage and teach you about his heart for the lost.

The Lost Sheep

> [4]"What man among you, if he has a hundred sheep and loses one of them, does not leave the ninety-nine in the wilderness and go after the one which is lost, [searching] until he finds it?
>
> [5]And when he has found it, he lays it on his shoulders, rejoicing.
>
> [6]And when he gets home, he calls together his friends and his neighbors, saying to them, 'Rejoice with me, because I have found my lost sheep!'
>
> [7]I tell you, in the same way there will be more joy in heaven over one sinner who repents than over ninety-nine righteous people who have no need of repentance."[57]

Luke 15:4–7 shows us an example of how much God values each person. Although the man in this parable had ninety-nine other sheep, he left them behind to search for the one that had wandered away from his flock. Once the man found it, he lovingly laid the sheep on his shoulders and returned home. Rejoicing, he called his friends together to share his happy news.

My heart of faith envisions the wayward sheep I am praying for, repentant and found—carried home by the Lord in this same loving manner. Jesus summarized this parable by comparing the found sheep with a repentant sinner. "I tell you, in the same way there will be more

---

57. Luke 15:4–7 (AMP)

joy in heaven over one sinner who repents than over ninety-nine righteous people who have no need of repentance."[58]

- What verse in this passage stands out to you?

- Is there someone in your life who needs a new or restored relationship with the Lord?

- If not, ask the Lord to show you a new activity where you, like Jesus, would have the opportunity to meet and befriend someone to share your faith with.

The Lost Coin

> [8]"Or what woman, if she has ten silver coins [each one equal to a day's wages] and loses one coin, does not light a lamp and sweep the house and search carefully until she finds it?
>
> [9]And when she has found it, she calls together her [women] friends and neighbors, saying, 'Rejoice with me, because I found the lost coin!'
>
> [10]In the same way, I tell you, there is joy in the presence of the angels of God over one sinner who repents [that is, changes his inner self—his old way of thinking, regrets past sins, lives his life in a way that proves repentance; and seeks God's purpose for his life]."[59]

Luke 15:8–10 reaffirms the lesson taught in the previous parable. As the woman diligently searched for her missing coin, we are reminded that every individual is valuable to God. The effort this

---

58. Luke 15:7 (AMP)
59. Luke 15:8–10 (AMP)

woman expended as she swept her house and searched for the coin inspires me to be persistent in praying for the spiritual restoration of my loved ones. I must faithfully keep praying until God answers my prayer.

Every individual is valuable to God.

Jesus compared her happiness over finding the coin to the joy in heaven over one lost soul that turns to God. "In the same way, I tell you, there is joy in the presence of the angels of God over one sinner who repents [that is, changes his inner self—his old way of thinking, regrets past sins, lives his life in a way that proves repentance; and seeks God's purpose for his life]."[60]

- As you pray in faith for someone who is not walking with the Lord, pray expectantly—with a celebration in mind!

- What close friends will you invite to rejoice with you?

The Lost Sons

> [11]Then He said, "A certain man had two sons.
>
> [12]The younger of them [inappropriately] said to his father, 'Father, give me the share of the property that falls to me.' So he divided the estate between them.

---

60. Luke 15:10 (AMP)

¹³A few days later, the younger son gathered together everything [that he had] and traveled to a distant country, and there he wasted his fortune in reckless and immoral living.

¹⁴Now when he had spent everything, a severe famine occurred in that country, and he began to do without and be in need.

¹⁵So he went and forced himself on one of the citizens of that country, who sent him into his fields to feed pigs.

¹⁶He would have gladly eaten the [carob] pods that the pigs were eating [but they could not satisfy his hunger], and no one was giving anything to him.

¹⁷But when he [finally] came to his senses, he said, 'How many of my father's hired men have more than enough food, while I am dying here of hunger!

¹⁸I will get up and go to my father, and I will say to him, "Father, I have sinned against heaven and in your sight.

¹⁹I am no longer worthy to be called your son; [just] treat me like one of your hired men."'

²⁰So he got up and came to his father. But while he was still a long way off, his father saw him and was moved with compassion for him, and ran and embraced him and kissed him.

²¹And the son said to him, 'Father, I have sinned against heaven and in your sight; I am no longer worthy to be called your son.'

²²But the father said to his servants, 'Quickly bring out the best robe [for the guest of honor] and put it on him; and give him a ring for his hand, and sandals for his feet.

[23]And bring the fattened calf and slaughter it, and let us [invite everyone and] feast and celebrate;

[24]for this son of mine was [as good as] dead and is alive again; he was lost and has been found.' So they began to celebrate.

[25]"Now his older son was in the field; and when he returned and approached the house, he heard music and dancing.

[26]So he summoned one of the servants and began asking what this [celebration] meant.

[27]And he said to him, 'Your brother has come, and your father has killed the fattened calf because he has received him back safe and sound.'

[28]But the elder brother became angry and deeply resentful and was not willing to go in; and his father came out and began pleading with him.

[29]But he said to his father, 'Look! These many years I have served you, and I have never neglected or disobeyed your command. Yet you have never given me [so much as] a young goat, so that I might celebrate with my friends;

[30]but when this [other] son of yours arrived, who has devoured your estate with immoral women, you slaughtered that fattened calf for him!'

[31]The father said to him, 'Son, you are always with me, and all that is mine is yours.

[32]But it was fitting to celebrate and rejoice, for this brother of yours was [as good as] dead and has begun to live. He was lost and has been found.'"[61]

---

61. Luke 15:11–32 (AMP)

In Luke 15:11–32, Jesus teaches with an example of family relationships—a father and his two sons. In this parable, we observe the father's faith as he willingly gave his younger son his portion of the inheritance. The word *prodigal* isn't actually found in the text but means "recklessly extravagant."[62] In context, you can see this is about the father giving lavishly, in addition to the *prodigal* referring to the extravagant spending or waywardness of one of the sons. Even though the son's request wasn't appropriate, and he wasn't mature enough to handle the money wisely, the father gave him what he wanted. I believe the father had faith that the consequences of his son's decisions would bring about lessons he needed to learn.

The son's humble repentance is what every parent of a wayward child hopes for.

After the younger son wastefully spent all his resources, he experienced the penalties of his immoral lifestyle—starvation and slave labor. Eventually, he came to his senses. Not only did he remember that his previous life was better, but he also humbly recognized that he no longer deserved to return to his former position in his father's household. He decided to return home to seek his father's forgiveness and ask to serve as one of his father's servants. The son's humble repentance is what every parent of a wayward child (including myself) hopes for.

Upon his return home, the son was graciously met by a joyous reunion with his dad. "But while he was still a long way off, his father saw him and was moved with compassion for him, and ran

---

62. *Merriam-Webster.com Dictionary*, s.v. "prodigal," accessed April 3, 2025, https://www.merriam-webster.com/dictionary/prodigal.

and embraced him and kissed him."[63] After they embraced, the father quickly told his servants to bring the son his best robe, a ring, and sandals. Then the father ordered his servants to prepare a feast in honor of his son's return.

The older son did not share his father's joy over his brother's return. He was angry and resentful that his father forgave his brother's transgressions, and he was jealous his father had never hosted a party for him. This passage was meant to show that both sons were lost, in their own way. The father went out to the older son and pleaded with him to join in the festivities for the younger son's return. "The father said to him, 'Son, you are always with me, and all that is mine is yours. But it was fitting to celebrate and rejoice, for this brother of yours was [as good as] dead and has begun to live. He was lost and has been found.'"[64]

- Which family member in this story can you most relate to?

- The younger son demonstrated impatience by demanding his inheritance. His actions remind me of how much I dislike waiting. Are there areas in your life where you feel impatient?

- The father did not argue or plead with his younger son regarding his demand for his inheritance. How would you have handled a similar situation?

---

63. Luke 15:20 (AMP)
64. Luke 15:31–32 (AMP)

- The father left the outcome of his son's poor decisions in God's hands. Are you completely trusting God to accomplish what is needed in the lives of those you care about?

- Do you have faith, like the father's, as he kept looking for his son's return?

- Do you have attitudes or behaviors similar to the older brother?

- Are you willing to forgive and accept those who have disappointed or hurt you?

This chapter has encouraged me to keep the faith as I wait for my loved ones to come to their senses and seek God's purpose for their lives. Like the father, I want to keep looking for the return of those who have wandered away from God and to continually pray they will find a right relationship with him. May the Lord help us to embrace God's faithfulness as we choose to trust the many promises in his Word.

Let It Flow, Sistahs!

by Mindy Cantrell

DO YOU SOMETIMES have days when life stinks and you struggle to stay positive? Don't worry, most of us do! Struggles hit. Difficulties pile up. Relationships become stressed. Overwhelm kicks in, and joy flies right out the window! With all the uncertainties of life these days, keeping a cheerful attitude can be challenging for sure.

When facing one of those days, I want to stay safely tucked in at home, away from all things causing my stress overload. I feel anxious and grumpy. I'm tempted with feelings of envy and dislike toward those who add to my bad day. Uh-oh.

I know kindness and compassion reign in God's world, but seriously, some days, I just can't.

Consequently, I don't feel like being kind, and I don't want to hear another word about politics, shootings, soaring prices, or anything fueling the hurt in my soul! I know kindness and compassion reign in God's world, but seriously, some days, I just can't. Do you relate?

Then, like me, do you find yourself indulging in unhealthy things such as crawling in bed and forgoing responsibilities? Watching too much TV? Or over-stuffing your face with comfort food—rich, creamy, dark chocolate drizzled over Blue Bell Homemade Vanilla ice cream. Or thick, stuffed crust pizza loaded with cheese. How about decadent chocolate brownies and bonbons? Yummy! Now that is soul food, right? What is your guilty pleasure on those tough days?

God Knows What We're Feeling

I was thinking, if all of us have days like that, then surely there is something positive we can do to brighten them. What are some encouraging things that would lift your spirit on days like this?

Did you know that because of our faithful God's great wisdom and love for us, he already knew we'd have days like this and provided some great remedies? Look what I found while reading his Word: "When you follow the desires of your sinful nature, the results are very clear: sexual immorality, impurity, lustful pleasures, idolatry, sorcery, hostility, quarreling, jealousy, outbursts of anger, selfish ambition, dissension, division, envy, drunkenness, wild parties, and other sins like these."[65]

Hmmm . . . that certainly covers my feelings and cravings on those difficult days, and some. How about you? God already knew all the feelings we'd experience and all our human attempts to feel better. It's not a surprise to him or a secret we keep from him that we feel this way. Or that we, as humans, desire these activities to make us feel better. So, what's the problem, then?

What's Wrong with Bad-Day Feelings?

God reveals the danger in the very next verse. He gives us a little warning to advise that though he knows we face temptations for these

---
65. Galatians 5:19–21 (NLT)

negative indulgences, we shouldn't *linger* in them. Then, he takes it one step further, stating that those who regularly practice these things will not inherit the kingdom of God!

Yikes! Pretty strong words there, aren't they? Well, stick with me here; I have good news!

Our great God, again, in his faithful love for us, provided answers to combat those feelings he doesn't want us to wallow in. As I read God's Word, I find more and more that when God asks us not to do something, he provides a sound alternative. Hooray!

As I read God's Word, I find more and more that when God asks us not to do something, he provides a sound alternative.

"But the Holy Spirit produces this kind of fruit in our lives: love, joy, peace, patience, kindness, goodness, faithfulness, gentleness, and self-control. There is no law against these things! Those who belong to Christ Jesus have nailed the passions and desires of their sinful nature to his cross and crucified them there. Since we are living by the Spirit, let us follow the Spirit's leading in every part of our lives. Let us not become conceited, or provoke one another, or be jealous of one another."[66]

Okay, message received. But how in the world do we go from feeling angry and needing appeasement to being patient and kind? Let's see what God says.

How to Offset Negative Feelings

"And now, dear brothers and sisters, one final thing. Fix your thoughts on what is true, and honorable, and right, and pure, and lovely, and admirable. Think about things that are excellent and worthy of praise."[67]

---

66. Galatians 5:22–26 (NLT)
67. Philippians 4:8 (NLT)

GATHER THE GOODNESS

Some Bible versions say to *dwell* on these things. In another use of the word, *dwell,* it can mean to "take up residence."[68] If you look at the original Greek verb Paul used in this passage, *logiozomai,*, it means "take into account" and "to determine, purpose, decide."[69] Drawing this all together, wouldn't it be nice if the whole world purposed and decided to reside in the above-listed fruit of the Spirit? Then the bad stuff would never happen.

Alas, not everyone wants to do the good or right thing, though. Some, in fact, want to do the *wrong* thing because it pleases our flesh, momentarily making us feel better. And each time we give ourselves over to the wrong thing, it gets harder and harder to see and do the *right* thing. And then we become stuck in the never-ending cycle of wrong. I don't know about you, but that doesn't sound like a place I want to be!

When we set our minds on it, we can think of endless kindnesses and beauty happening around our world.

The Best Solution

So, what do we do? We do what God instructs us—we focus our minds on whatever is true, honorable, right, pure, lovely, admirable, with moral excellence and praiseworthy. You know, things like a beautiful newborn baby, a flamboyant flower rising up in the middle of a brown field, a sudden cool breeze on a hot day, a kind mechanic benevolently fixing the single mom's car. What else can you think of?

---

68. *Merriam-Webster.com Dictionary*, s.v. "dwell," accessed March 6, 2025, https://www.merriam-webster.com/dictionary/dwell
69. "G3049 - logizomai – *Strong's Greek Lexicon* (KJV)," Blue Letter Bible, accessed April 13, 2025, https://www.blueletterbible.org/lexicon/g3049/kjv/tr/0-1/

You see, when we set our minds on it, we can think of endless kindnesses and beauty happening around our world. Joy-filled goodness we can concentrate on—participate in. Lifting our spirits and restoring hope in our hearts. And on those days when it's just too dark to see, we can ask the Holy Spirit to reveal his light-giving benevolence, dispelling our darkness.

So, what do you say? Let's renew our minds and hearts by focusing on these meaningful moments. Then we can move right into kind, hope-filled thoughts and take up residence! What are some uplifting words and events you can think of? Make yourself a list and start checking them off, one by one.

When our minds are residing in those heartwarming thoughts, we find love, joy, peace, patience, kindness, goodness, faithfulness, gentleness, and self-control begin to flow into us. And then flow out onto those around us. It just takes a little practice, and before you know it, the fruit of the Spirit becomes a natural part of our character. And thereby refreshing our desire to practice faithfulness, even on those difficult days.

Just like that warm cloak, the Spirit's fruit will comfort us and outfit us with what we need to keep going, no matter the season we're in.

So, let's embrace them, joyfully putting them on like a warm cloak in the middle of a frigid snowstorm. Just like that warm cloak, the Spirit's fruit will comfort us and outfit us with what we need to keep going, no matter the season we're in. And before you know it, this beautiful fruit will be flowing out of us and outfitting those around us.

Let them flow, Sistahs. Let them flow!

Surrender

by Joni Topper

Surrender to God's faithfulness; you
    will not find regret.
Take him at his Holy Word; he's never left you yet.
When all you see is trouble, you do not know the way,
Surrender to God's faithfulness; walk
    with him through the day.

When heartbreak is your constant
    friend, you will not be alone.
When pain has gripped your body,
    he'll carry you back home.
When no one seems to understand,
    his faithfulness you'll find.
When you let go, he'll take your hand;
    you'll find him always kind.

If cold is the season, and darkness fills the air,
Just open up his story and find yourself a chair.

A little time spent pondering the Spirit of the Lord.
Close your eyes and talk to him;
    you'll find a great reward.
The saints who've gone before you
    will tell their stories true;
When you have listened to them, you'll
    know just what to do.

Surrender to God's faithfulness; you
    will not find regret.
Take him at his Holy Word; he's never left you yet.
When all you see is trouble, you do not know the way,
Surrender to God's faithfulness; walk
    with him through the day.

Yes, surrender to God's faithfulness, walk
    with him through the day.

Safe with My Father

by Joni Topper

Let us hold tightly without wavering to the hope we affirm, for God can be trusted to keep his promise.

Hebrews 10:23 (NLT)

I HAVE FEW MEMORIES of playing with my dad. That's not to say Dad did not play. He played with everyone everywhere and often got into mischief, even as an adult. But he was a man's man, so his adventures didn't often include things that held interest for little girls.

Our family also took very few vacations. If we did, they were usually camping trips. I remember sleeping at a roadside park. Mom and Dad slept in the back of the station wagon. All three of us girls slept on cots beside the car. Mom and Dad left the back window open so they could see and hear what we were doing. In the morning, Dad made our breakfast on the park grill. The older ones consisted of cinder bricks arranged to hold a grate in place. Dad built a fire under it and cooked with a cast iron skillet. We had some tasty meals prepared on those makeshift cookouts.

One of my favorite vacations was a rare occasion when we stayed in a hotel. There was even a swimming pool. My parents lounged around the pool. Walking around in swimsuits with soft drinks and big round balls and floaties made me feel like I was on the set of a movie. I was about six years old. After getting used to this glamorous setting, I decided to try something the other kids were doing. With great confidence, I jumped from the side of the pool into a brightly colored inner tube. *Easy peasy,* I thought.

My aim was spot on, but my decision-making process fell short. The ring I jumped into was large. I was small, and I swooshed right through the middle of that thing and sank straight to the bottom. Not yet knowing how to swim, I remember looking up from the bottom of the pool to see the bright red and blue tube above me.

Before I had time to realize I was in danger, my dad jumped into the pool and pulled me to safety. As a child, instinctively, I knew this was what fathers do. They rescue their children.

Fast-Forward Ten Years

An intruder entered our home in the middle of the night. I awakened to realize that he'd been beside my bed, touching me in private places. My dad was out of town that night. Later, his anger ate at him over the incident. He worked in law enforcement at that time, and the idea that his own home could be a target, just like any other home, did not sit well with him. For the first time, Dad faced the reality that he could not protect his children from everything evil in the world.

The worst thing stolen from me that night was peace. I could not sleep after this incident. Safety seemed like something far off, just a little out of reach. For several weeks, bedtime became unsettling. I knew my dad felt awful about what happened, yet he could do little to help me. Because I could tell he felt helpless, I wanted to keep my discomfort to myself. I didn't want to add to his angst, and besides, he was not responsible for what happened anyway.

I had asked Jesus to be my Savior as a seven-year-old girl. I knew that my heavenly Father promised to be with me always. In fact, the Bible said he would be with me until the end of the earth. The songs we sang at church talked about trusting and obeying, and they clearly promised that in doing so, we would be happy in Jesus. I was trying to figure out how all this might connect and help relieve my fear every night at bedtime.

God offers hope but its power is tied to my own willingness to accept it.

One night, I decided to try to find answers. Adults in my life talked of finding them in the Bible. I opened mine to read a story of David, but it led me to more anxiety as I read about him hiding from Saul, who was determined to kill him. *The book of Psalms might be more reassuring,* I thought as I flipped to a different book of the Bible. My understanding of Scripture made these words jump off the page as I read them because I knew they were the words of David. The same David I'd just read about, who was hiding in a cave, trying to preserve his life. "I will both lie down in peace, and sleep; For You alone, O Lord, make me dwell in safety."[70]

There it was. The answer to my quest for peace lay in David's willingness to trust God. Not his confidence in man. He decided to take God at his word and accept his faithful promise to provide peace. The choice was mine—*is* mine. The choice is always mine. God offers hope but its power is tied to my own willingness to accept it.

---

70. Psalm 4:8 (NKJV)

Did I want to follow David's example and lie down in peace or not? My choice. The gift was available—is always available—but God never forced me to accept it.

Fast-Forward Another Eight Years

When my first marriage ended, I was twenty-four years old. Devasted by the situation, I also found out a week after divorce proceedings began that I was pregnant. Around me, people made comments about my situation. Some of them suggested having another baby at that time might not be a good plan.

Only God knew how relieved I was that my little girl would have a sibling during her childhood. Part of my heartache about the divorce was because I wanted my daughter to have a sibling close enough in age that she could play and bond with while they grew up. While this pregnancy was not planned, I knew it was the answer to my heart's desire.

The day my baby was born, while I waited for my turn in surgery, my dad cried. It was one of the few times I ever saw him cry. I'm not sure what brought his tears. While my dad offered me important things, I'd learned by then that my *heavenly* Father was my rock.

The Years That Followed

God's faithfulness has been on display over and over through the years. Fortunately, my dad provided a model of what a child can expect from a loving father. Dad taught me that a father looks out for his children, that he can create wonderful experiences at places as simple as a roadside park, but that he can't do the things a heavenly Father can do. He can't mend a heart or guarantee peace.

God provides opportunities and good reasons for us to accept his faithful offers. He's never disappointed me. He's been faithful in protecting my heart in grief, betrayal, frustration, and in my own shortcomings. Yes, I'm holding tightly to the hope he promised.

The Land of Rainbows

by Lisa-Anne Wooldridge

*I*T WAS RAINING sideways. Even in the middle of the day, the sky was twilight-dark, and the wind was fierce. If gloomy had a picture in the dictionary, it would be the view outside my window. All the papers were full of bad news, and the talking heads on television droned on about the dire state of things until I switched it off, maybe for good. God had spoken to my heart that morning with a simple, soft verse, but I admit, my outlook was still as brooding as the weather.

In His Light

I locked myself away with a cup of tea and the last of the pumpkin muffins. I hoped relocating to a cozy spot in my home would help me weather the spiritual storm brewing inside. I needed quiet, peace, and reassurance, but I also knew I needed a perspective change. The verse that was meant to guide me earlier in the day wasn't landing, and I knew it was because I wasn't *listening*.

The weather and my mood were so in sync that it actually thundered when I started to pray. "The world is a scary place right now . . ."

GATHER THE GOODNESS

Rumble, rumble. "How are we meant to live our lives with everything going on?" *Grumble, grumble.* Okay, that last bit was me; I can't blame the storm for that one.

A flash of lightning lit up the sky and my room, momentarily brightening the landscape around me. The trees stood out in sharp relief on the hillside, nearly white with light instead of their usual emerald green. In a snap, the darkness fell again and seemed even heavier than before.

We See Light

I sat quietly, knowing my mood needed God's touch. I've often pondered that God can see in the dark, but we only see in the light. Darkness isn't a problem for God. He *is* light. If we abide in him, we can "see" in the dark too. I'd survived other storms. No matter how frightening, he'd never left me on my own. Shoot, I'd never even caught Jesus sleeping in the boat! His faithfulness always carried me through, one way or another, to the other side of the squall.

God can see in the dark, but we only see in the light.

Then there were the rainbows. Vivid, beautiful reminders of all his promises. Whether actual rainbows showed up in the sky or people showed up in my life like colorful, candy-coated gifts from above, he made sure I could taste and see his goodness and rest in his faithfulness and love.[71]

I buried my face in a pillow and let the tears come. "Remind me of your faithfulness, God. Don't let my soul forget a single one of your

---

71. Psalm 34:8

benefits."[72] And he did. Memories of hard times and desperate days came to mind, times when I faced trauma or tragedy. There was no pain in the reliving, though, because he'd held me up and walked with me through all of them. No matter how dark the night or how strong the sorrows, he'd carried me and cared for me. I smiled through my tears, but then he asked me a question, and it lit a fire in me.

"So, what makes this time different?"

In Him Is the Fountain of Life

I'd been overwhelmed by the sheer volume of bad things going on in the world. Negative messages designed to make us feel hopeless and upside-down. God knew I was vulnerable that day, and the weather outside wouldn't help my state of mind. The seed he'd planted in my thoughts was beginning to grow. So, what did make this time different? I flipped open my notebook to look at the verse I'd jotted down from memory. "They feast on the abundance of your house, and you give them drink from the river of your delights. For with you is the fountain of life; in your light do we see light."[73]

How were we supposed to live our lives? God's answer seemed to be the same as always. He was the source, the fountain of life. I can be satisfied in his presence and drink from the river of his delights, and then, well, I'll see the light. I'll be in the light, which makes seeing a lot easier! No matter what storm was raging around me, my faithful Father had prepared a feast for me.

"Okay, I'll do that. I'll sit here and enjoy your company until the storm passes. I'll wait it out. Hit me with that delightful river thing." I closed my eyes and tucked my blanket, waiting for the familiar peace to wash over me. Nothing happened. I squeezed my eyes shut a little

---

72. Psalm 103:2
73. Psalm 36:8–9 (ESV)

tighter, hoping I'd switch over to sunshine mode. Outside, the wind picked up and rattled my windows. This storm didn't seem in any hurry to leave.

In the Midst

God seemed to be playing "But wait, there's more" with me. I had a feeling I was being offered two lessons for the price of one. (Just pay shipping and handling!) I checked the weather app on my phone. We weren't just having a storm; it was a whole atmospheric river, a deluge that decided to park itself right over our heads and stay for a while. Just like the storms outside, the weighty troubles of the world also seemed to be settling in for an extended visit.

"Okay, I get it. I'm ready and willing to learn whatever you want me to know because it's pretty uncomfortable here, and you know I'd rather just do the thing and walk the way you want me to go." Pretty sure God raised an eyebrow at that, but thankfully, he let it pass. "What am I missing? This feels like a long, hard journey."

My memory was nudged. "Remember those who wandered in the desert." Oh, yes. They had a long, hard trip and a whirlwind too—a huge tornado that stayed right with them. The cloud by day gave them shade, and the fire by night took the chill off. I opened my Bible to the book of Numbers. Then I saw it. I saw *him* in the text. Lightning struck again, filling my mind with brilliant light.

Face to Face

His faithfulness was greater than I ever knew, to his people then and to his people now. I copied the words of the text to treasure. "For you, O Lord, are seen face to face, and your cloud stands over them and you go before them, in a pillar of cloud by day and in a pillar of fire by night."[74] God was with his people in the middle of the unending storm, so much so they could make eye contact. In several literal text versions of the Bible (such as the New American Standard Bible), it's translated as "eye to eye."[75]

We are safe in the eye of the storm because we are the apple of his eye.

No matter what, I can see eye to eye with God by trusting his faithfulness and following the path he's carved out. We are safe in the eye of the storm because we are the apple of his eye. He sent a double rainbow a few minutes later to remind me.

What a way to live!

---

74. Numbers 14:14 (ESV)
75. New American Standard Bible (NASB), Num. 14:14 (The Lockman Foundation, 2020).

Your unfailing love, O Lord, is as vast as the heavens;
your faithfulness reaches beyond the clouds.
Your righteousness is like the mighty mountains,
your justice like the ocean depths.
You care for people and animals alike, O Lord.
How precious is your unfailing love, O God!

Psalm 36:5–7 (NLT)

When the Mountain Won't Move

by Betty Predmore

SOMETIMES, LIFE GETS so heavy it feels like a mountain that won't move. You want to have the faithfulness that is mentioned time and again in God's Word. But the struggle is real, and often it's hard to hold on. Becoming a single mom with four kids and wondering how I was going to make it was one of those times in my life when I almost allowed myself to be crushed under the weight of that mountain.

It reminds me of a passage in Scripture where Jesus told the disciples, "Have faith in God. Truly I say to you, whoever says to this mountain, 'Be taken up and thrown into the sea,' and does not doubt in his heart, but believes that what he says will come to pass, it will be done for him. Therefore I tell you, whatever you ask in prayer, believe that you have received it, and it will be yours."[76]

---

[76]. Mark 11:22–24 (ESV)

Rescued by Belief

Jesus's words whispered around in my heart, rising to the surface when I felt at my lowest. They told me not to doubt. There was a reminder that my faith was the lifeline that could pull me up the side of that mountain to the mountaintop, where hope is found. All I had to do was believe.

I held on to those words with a tight grasp. I pulled myself up that rope, one knot at a time. As I did, that huge mountain got smaller and smaller. As my mountain decreased in stature, my faith increased, filling my heart with assuredness that there is nothing I cannot overcome when God is with me. And he is always with me.

He was there to walk alongside me each of my days as I worked, maintained a home, and raised my children on my own. He wouldn't walk away when the battle was tough nor disappear when my doubt tried to surface. He was the constant in my life who would see me through.

He Never Leaves Us

When we are caught in the darkness, feeling lost, doubting our next steps, God is right there. Knowing and believing that makes all the difference. Trusting in the promises of his Word is like the brightest beacon on the darkest night.

Does fear have you bound in chains? *Have faith.* Are you buried in grief? *Have faith.* Are anger and frustration robbing you of your joy? *Have faith.* Do you doubt yourself, isolate yourself from others, or worry about your tomorrows? *Have faith.*

Believing When You Cannot See

The mountain may be positioned right in front of you at this moment, and it may feel as though it can't be moved. Maybe you can't see around it to what is beyond. But when you put your trust in Jesus, you don't have to see what is ahead. You can simply know that your mountain will become a molehill when you march with God's army. Scripture tells us that our faithfulness comes not from seeing but from believing what we cannot see.

Trusting God with the unseen is the true definition of faith.

We believe because God's Word tells us it is so. We place our hope in God, trusting him with the mountains that seem too big to deal with. Trusting God with the unseen is the true definition of faith.

"For we walk by faith, not by sight."[77]

Those impossible mountains are not impossible to God. He who can part the sea, bring sight to a blind man, cleanse the skin of a leper, and raise a man from the dead can certainly move our mountains. His faithfulness inspires *me* to be faithful!

---

77. 2 Corinthians 5:7 (ESV)

A Tapestry of Faithfulness

by Joanie Shawhan

Faithful, faithful the shuttle flies
In the Master's hand,
Loom's strands yet to be interlaced,
An unfinished masterpiece buried in the fibers,
Threads of faithfulness woven in the heart of God.

His faithfulness gleaned from mother's knee:
Hymns, rote prayers,
Lives of saints gone to eternal reward,
Biblical truths, Ten Commandments,
Jesus's birth, death, and resurrection.

Immersed in life skills with six siblings:
Squabbles, sharing, negotiating,
Catching fireflies, playing freeze tag,
Skates with keys, scraped knees,
Riding bikes until streetlights glimmered.

Hayrides in the pasture at the grandparents' farm,
Running with cousins, plucking apples and grapes,
Grandma's sugar cookies fresh from the jar,
Grandpa's voice bellowing,
"Stay away from the bull."

Enthralled by books, crafts, and teen idols,
Piano, guitar, choir practice,
Cheering our team under stadium lights,
Store checker and hospital candy striper—
Precursor to God's calling.

Faithful guidance through nursing school,
Lifelong friendships
Forged through dorm life and exams,
Attending to patients:
Medications, treatments, spiritual care.

Back and forth the shuttle of faithfulness passed,
Through betrayals, heartaches, joys,
Friendships guided and protected,
Unexpected alliances
Chosen by an unseen hand.

Mature mentors teaching the Word of God,
Service, fellowship, and the power of prayer.
Holy Spirit, guide through this world,
Comforter, helper,
Counselor, friend.

His patient untangling of difficult trials:
Caregiving, grief, shattered dreams,
Through cancer and chemo.
Is survival possible?
Yes—his faithfulness never ceased.

Family heartbreak—the loss of a sister
Taken too soon by stage four cancer.
Hopes crushed in the dark of night,
A whisper—walk her home,
Yet his faithfulness prevailed.

A new season emerged,
Wisdom gleaned through life's lessons,
Writing spiritual truths and cancer survival,
Coached by industry peers and mentors
To published author of articles, devotions, and books.

Celebrations gathered around the table,
Meals mingled with laughter and joy,
Fellow lovers of books and writing,
Bible studies and intercession,
Treasured friendships—every one.

Sometimes glimpsing an obscure design,
An array of tangled threads,
I ask the Master weaver,
"Will the tapestry be beautiful?"
"Oh yes—one day, you will see.

"Grace covers every imperfection,
My faithfulness woven throughout the design
Entwines us together for all eternity."
Faithful, faithful the shuttle flies
In the Master's hand.

Gentleness

Robot Vacs and Human Hearts

by Hally J. Wells

So, as God's own chosen people, who are holy [set apart, sanctified for His purpose] and well-beloved [by God Himself], put on a heart of compassion, kindness, humility, gentleness, and patience [which has the power to endure whatever injustice or unpleasantness comes, with good temper].

COLOSSIANS 3:12 (AMP)

I'M NOT A fan of technology, and I have no interest in my house being smart. I prefer my dumb, old-school methods and will gladly do things the hard way if the alternative requires learning a lot of new techie tidbits.

My husband sees things differently. So, for Christmas last year, he blessed me with a robotic vacuum. Blasted! He'd gotten it 50 percent off and was certain it would be a big timesaver—particularly, given the fact that we'd replaced our worn carpet with laminate, and we share our home with a barking, shedding beagle. I grumbled my gratefulness and was happy-ish to have the new toy if he would figure it out, map the route, and set the run timer for me. That was probably not the reaction he'd hoped for.

I knew of others who had these handy household devices. We called ours Robot Rosie. While I wasn't enthusiastic about my Christmas gift, I have grown to appreciate Ms. Rosie and her contributions to my home's hygiene. However, sometimes, if things aren't just as she expects or remembers, or if they're not arranged as they should be, Rosie finds herself getting knocked around, thrown off course, disoriented, and spinning in circles. At times like those, I'm sure she'd like to turn tail and head right back to her little space in my laundry room.

You know, when we invite folks to church, to join our small groups, to share lunch after Sunday services, or into a conversation before worship, we ought to keep Rosie in mind. When Robot Rosie took up residence in our house, we showed her around. We gave her a map, so to speak. We showed her what to expect. And we've tried to ensure that she doesn't run into challenges or trials that might make her retreat or sour her experience at 555 Dirty Floor Lane.

When we help them to feel more comfortable and confident, we create a space for them to reach out rather than retreat.

Likewise, when we welcome new people into our faith families, we bless them by making those experiences easy and without stress. We serve God when we prepare others for little bumps in the road, address their concerns, answer questions about the unknown faith places they'll be visiting, and offer guidance that will help them move easily through new territory. And, when we help them to feel more comfortable and confident, we create a space for them to reach out rather than retreat.

That is the nature of gentleness—the offer of a welcoming and affirming handshake, the promise of a soft landing, and the assurance of safe passage from a fellow traveler. When we provide a gentle place for those who are seeking, we plant seeds on his behalf.

Heavenly Father, help me show gentleness to seekers and searchers. Give me the words and actions that, when shared with others, will help them to find and follow you.

Stained-Glass Love

by Lisa-Anne Wooldridge

The girl I was sat by a stream
And prayed for the boy I'd marry,
And in my heart was born the dream
Of the gentleness he'd carry.
I rushed, all laughter and thunder,
Around a corner one day,
Straight into the man of wonder—
Somehow, I knew his name.
He reached to keep me from falling
His eyes were full of grace,
His careful hands gently held me,
His tenderness kept me in place.
He was strength constrained,
So very smart and sweet,
But it was his spirit of gentleness
That swept me off my feet.
He kept me grounded,
When I got carried away—
With him, I was surrounded
By a love that made me safe.

I could hear the shouting in my mind,
The day I got married.
It was a joyful sound so loud
I was afraid it carried

184 | GATHER THE GOODNESS

Through the pews and down the aisle,
Like a flower girl before me.
And then I saw him smile,
This gentle man God made for me.
Oh, how I wanted just to run,
Forsake tradition and decorum.
My father's steady arm held strong,
But my heart made a beeline straight for him.

I was a wild and lively girl,
Sound, color, light unrestrained.
He was a quiet man—my whole world;
He was the window, and I was the pane.
His stretched-out hand reached for me,
And all my bright, fractured pieces became
A vivid illustration—a redemption story,
Where all my pieces fit in his frame.
I met him at the altar that day
Where faith was singing hope's refrain.
A stained-glass love flashed before me,
Faith, hope, love—these three remain.

We came together under a window
made of tinted glass and stone
That shone the light of heaven—
Hearts entwined; God enthroned.
He brought what fruit I was missing
As an offering from the Lord
And taught me in the whispering
That gentleness is its own reward.

Gentleness on Display

by Joni Topper

But the wisdom from above is first pure, then peaceable, gentle, open to reason, full of mercy and good fruits, impartial and sincere. And a harvest of righteousness is sown in peace by those who make peace.

JAMES 3:17–18 (ESV)

WE SAT IN an ER waiting for someone to take my friend Macy back for an exam. She had been in pain for days. This was her third attempt to figure out why. She tried distracting herself. "Did I ever tell you how I became roommates with Julie, the lady I live with?"

"No. Have you known her long?" I replied.

My sick friend continued the story, explaining that she and Julie had known each other since they were kids. "We did not like each other. We were so mean. We threw things at each other and did not get along at all." While she said this, a smile grew across her pained face.

GATHER THE GOODNESS

Macy has been on her own since she was sixteen years old. She applied for emancipation because there was so much turmoil at home. She went to work in the kitchen at the local nursing home while she finished high school.

"One day, as I entered the building to work, my boss told another worker to get out of there and never come back." She raised her eyebrows. "I got a new job that day, but I could not start my training until someone was hired to take my place." Then, she grimaced, "The person who applied for the job and got it was Julie. I had to train her."

Macy said she recognized that Julie lacked confidence in herself. "I took her in. With every bit of gentleness I could muster, I encouraged her. 'You can do this.' I explained each detail of the job with kindness." She said she even surprised herself. "I knew that if we were going to work together, it needed to be peaceful."

Macy understood life in a stressed household, she said. She knew the people at that nursing home needed the staff to be the best versions of themselves while at work. She knew being mean to Julie would not translate into kindness for the residents.

Julie took her cue. She learned her job and returned the gentle attitude. Several years later, when Macy found herself in great need of a place to live with her three children, Julie opened her doors. "We've learned to enjoy the better qualities in each other," Macy said.

God's Word offers us a recipe to avoid strife in every situation we face.

Macy explained that over the next several years, she was able to encourage Julie to apply for other jobs in the nursing home, assuring her each time that she was capable of doing the necessary work. "When we were kids, I never dreamed that we would be friends someday," she said, shaking her head. "Our friendship has resulted in me and my children having a good, safe place to live."

It turned out that the things Macy did not like about Julie when they were younger were actually behaviors formed largely because of insecurities.

Often, when we step back from hostile relationships and view them from a place of mercy and a desire to be reasonable, we experience them very differently. God's Word offers us a recipe to avoid strife in every situation we face.

Lord, give me the ability to see relationships through your gentle eyes. Help me remember that the best outcomes of conflict result in actions that honor you.

Let your gentle spirit [your graciousness, unselfishness, mercy, tolerance, and patience] be known to all people. The Lord is near.

Philippians 4:5 (amp)

Gentleness Is Power

by Sandy Lipsky

A soft answer turns away wrath, but a harsh word stirs up anger. The tongue of the wise commends knowledge, but the mouths of fools pour out folly. The eyes of the Lord are in every place, keeping watch on the evil and the good. A gentle tongue is a tree of life, but perverseness in it breaks the spirit.

Proverbs 15:1–4 (esv)

I WAS MAD. IF anger produced smoke in my brain and escaped through my ears, my bedroom would have triggered a fire alarm. My family was used to my frequent angry outbursts. Though I felt ashamed, I could not control them despite trying.

While I was growing up, Saturdays were for chores. Mom made sure we finished our tasks before any fun. After a hectic week as a high school sophomore, I needed sleep. Mom understood and granted me permission to sleep until noon.

GATHER THE GOODNESS

The next morning, I heard Mom call up the stairs at 8:00 a.m. I rolled over, covering my head with a pillow, reminding myself I had permission to sleep late.

Mom gently called up the stairs a few more times. My fury grew, spreading like a forest fire in a field of chaff. After her fourth or fifth call, I leaped from bed, stomped downstairs, and started a tirade before reaching the kitchen.

Mom stepped back, shrugged her shoulders, and with a timid smile, said, "Dad has a surprise for you." She gestured toward the screen door, pointing at our garage. My gaze followed her hand. I didn't understand what she wanted me to see, so I pushed open the door and huffed down the steps.

Riding a bike represented freedom to me. Pedaling down the roads of our small town and into the nearby countryside was my way of coping with intense emotions and boredom, and it provided time alone to think. It was also how I avoided chores. For years, I had begged my parents for a ten-speed bike because my siblings both had one. As the youngest of three, I was accustomed to waiting for things, but that did not stop me from pestering my parents about it.

Near the garage, my dad stood looking at me with his hand on my grayish-green bicycle. It looked different. As I checked out the new ten-speed style seat and curved handlebars with gears, Dad spoke gently. He described step by step how he made the changes and hoped I liked them. My father, in secret, had transformed my "baby" bike into a cool teenager ride.

His gentle response to my initial fury melted my hardened core.

Dad and I were too much alike to get along when I was a kid. He took the brunt of my childish anger. But as I looked at my transformed bike, something started to shift inside me. My heart softened, and I saw my dad as a thoughtful, unselfish, and generous soul. His abundant and undeserved gift to me showed he had listened to my pleas. His gentle response to my initial fury melted my hardened core.

Proverbs 15:1 says, "A soft answer turns away wrath, but a harsh word stirs up anger." My father's gentle response was a living testament to this wisdom. In his quiet, loving way, he diffused my anger and turned a moment of fury into one of gratitude and love. His actions illustrated the profound impact of kindness and patience, bringing to life the Scripture's timeless advice.

Father, thank you for the transforming power of a gentle answer.

Gentle Words

by Julia Thompson

"THE WATER LOOKS so blue today," Hannah commented as she and another counselor paddled across the lake.

"It does," Liz agreed, "I'm so glad you suggested this. I needed some peace after this last group came through!"

Hannah lifted her oar from the water, placed it across the canoe, and turned to face Liz. "Did you have a tough group of kids to work with this last time?" she asked.

"No. There was only one girl who, well . . . the real problem was how a certain situation was handled."

Hannah recalled hearing about the disagreement between two junior-highers that became a physical altercation. "Was it involving the girl who had been bullied so badly?"

Liz rested her oar. "Sometimes . . ." She paused, then continued in a fluster of words, "I question the judgment of our leader. I don't understand why she didn't see the problem before they actually hit and hurt each other!"

Hannah nodded in agreement.

Liz continued, "Ms. Carol seems intelligent and sincere, but there are times I don't understand her ways."

Suddenly a catfish splashed inches from the canoe. Hannah giggled as Liz wiped water from her face. "The dangers of camp life, right? All laughs aside, Liz, you seem genuinely concerned. Maybe you should talk with Ms. Carol about it."

"Maybe I will." Liz pondered her options. A loud beep from her cell phone sounded rudely out of place on the quiet lake. "Ugh. This time went by so fast! We have only an hour before the next group arrives."

Two oars hit the water simultaneously.

☙

Later, a cool breeze graced the steamy camp. It flowed through the screens of the dining hall, where Ms. Carol stood silently counting chairs in a row before her. Liz carried the last two chairs in from the porch. Why couldn't she find the courage to speak to her boss? Frustrated, she dropped the chairs to the floor, then pushed them toward Ms. Carol. As they screeched across the floor, the camp leader caught them and placed them in the next row.

"Well, looks like we're ready. Thanks for your help, Liz."

Liz nodded and headed for the door.

"Counselor, do you have a minute? I think we need to talk."

With a heavy sigh, Liz turned toward her.

"Something is bothering you," Ms. Carol said. "How can I help?"

"I don't get you!" The words burst from Liz. "You seem so nice, but how could you stand by and do nothing while a child was bullied until it came to fists flying? I don't understand how you could not see a problem like this coming!" Liz threw her arms in the air, then dropped them in frustration.

Ms. Carol stared at the young counselor in shock, then sank into the nearest chair. "I don't know what to say, Liz."

"Well . . . well . . . I think if you're going to stay here as camp leader, you need to lead! Be aware so your counselors don't have to console girls with black eyes and pummeled hearts." Liz knew she had gone too far.

Ms. Carol's face was blotchy red, and it was obvious she was on the cusp of tears.

"That's all I have to say, I guess," Liz mumbled and hurried out the door, her limbs weak from the confrontation.

꿍

One week later, Hannah found herself in similar straits. After dinner, while Hannah cleaned the tables, Ms. Carol trudged into the dining hall with arms full of art supplies. *It's now or never*, Hannah thought. "Um . . . Ms. Carol, may I talk to you for a minute?"

"Sure, Hannah. Let me empty my arms."

Hannah took a deep breath and prayed, "Lord, please help me find the right words."

"Come. Sit. What's up?" Ms. Carol pulled up a chair from a table.

"Well, I want to say this right. Last week, we had a problem with two girls from the group. I have a sixth grader in my group who is being bullied. I've intervened, I've explained it's wrong to treat someone like that, but it continues. I don't know what else to do. I know you care for our campers. I'm looking for advice."

Ms. Carol relaxed her shoulders and let her hands fall to her lap, the fingers white from where they had been clasped tightly. "Hannah, I was prepared for different words. I appreciate your coming to me about the problem. About the last bullying incident, I neglected to see a problem until I had to place myself in the middle of four flying fists. Had I known sooner, I would have spoken to the girls and taken corrective measures."

A squeak from the screen door made them both turn to see who was coming inside.

No one was there, so Ms. Carol continued, "If you leave me the names I need, I will talk to the girls and try to put a stop to this behavior. Anything else, Hannah?"

"No, ma'am. Thanks for listening."

"Sure thing." With that, Ms. Carol spread the art supplies across the table, and Hannah finished her cleaning.

※

It was evening when Liz and Hannah chatted about the day as they arranged the campfire wood.

"I talked with Ms. Carol today about the bullying situations," Hannah shared.

"Yeah, I know. I heard," Liz said.

"How?" Hannah asked in surprise.

"Well, I actually heard you talking to her. I was outside the door."

"Wait, you eavesdropped on our conversation?"

"That wasn't my plan, but I did overhear you. In fact, I have to say, Hannah, I was shocked to hear how you spoke to our camp leader."

"Liz, I was trying to be gentle! Didn't I do that? The conversation is a bit blurry because my nerves were jumping all over the place."

"You did exactly that, Hannah. You made the same point as I did when I spoke to her, but you used kind words. You were gentle." Liz looked down at her feet. "I'm glad you didn't hear how I spoke to her. How did you find the words to be so careful?"

Hannah added the last log to the pile as she explained, "Perhaps you've just forgotten what our last discussion around the campfire was about? Gentleness and kindness didn't come from me. I was still upset about the bullying going on. Those words I spoke, Liz? They were fruit." Hannah sat down next to her friend. "I'm so grateful Jesus helped me. Remember? When we belong to Jesus and allow his Holy Spirit to work in us, we can see fruit like gentleness and kindness growing in us. We can see, and others can see it showing up in what we do and say."

Liz shoulder-bumped her friend, then quietly shared, "I should have prayed before I confronted her."

"Liz,"—Hannah smiled—"It's all about keeping in touch with God, walking in step with his Holy Spirit daily. This will make us 'fruity.'"

They laughed. The fire caught hold of the logs, but it was more than flames that warmed them.

Leaning into God's Gentleness

by Becki James

Then Jesus said, "Come to me, all of you who are weary and carry heavy burdens, and I will give you rest. Take my yoke upon you. Let me teach you, because I am humble and gentle at heart, and you will find rest for your souls. For my yoke is easy to bear, and the burden I give you is light."

MATTHEW 11:28–30 (NLT)

THIS VERSE HIT me in a tender spot. *That is me, Lord,* I sighed. *I am tired.* A soft reply arose in my spirit—*That is why you are here.*

Accepting that response took a while. Slowing down is hard for me. I am a roll-up-your-sleeves-and-do-it girl. My energy level is high, and I am a natural leader. I love people. My days open like a revolving door for those God brings to me. I enjoy the adventure of busyness and never imagined that pace would lead to exhaustion.

A red flag should have alerted me when I resorted to a large-blocked, year-at-a-glance calendar tacked beside my Keurig. Color coding events seemed fun—even satisfying. Orange for school events. Pink for the small group I led. Blue and green spattered travel months as a pro men's basketball chaplain. Brown for the youth mentoring program. Oh, and a rainbow of activities for church, appointments, and the ten people living in my home. Lastly, a yellow ring circled the cross-country moving date on month six—with three families in tow. Coffee anyone? Yes, please.

    Daily, I managed the schedule, ending each day with a faint, inky squiggle of completion. I treasured my work, but fulfilling everything by the deadline drained my body and spirit. My usual perkiness waned. *Lord, get me through this*, I prayed. Weariness set in. But this fatigue stemmed from good things. Good people. Good ministry. I found myself longing to be on the other side, in a place where someone came alongside me.

    The big moving day arrived. A caravan of vehicles carried fourteen souls to our new home—the temporary family compound. Months passed. Everyone settled into their own places. Then, life slowed—way—down. My calendar went blank. The bright pens remained in a dark storage tote. I felt lost in this foreign reality. I wondered why God had removed everything familiar to me.

When I am overwhelmed, God gently bids me, come.

    But God was not interested in recreating my past. His gentle blueprint unfolded with teaching me to rest in him. He offered the familiarity of his companionship alone—far from the busyness I was accustomed to. Now, with ample time to reflect, I began to see his foresight for my well-being.

    God calls the weary. I love that. When I am overwhelmed, God gently bids me, *come*. He seeks me. Worn. Ragged. I am still the object of his affection. He acknowledges the burdens I carry, offsets the load, and offers relief in his presence. Unlike human interaction, God's fellowship is grounded in divine tenderness. His whole nature expresses the comprehension and love for human frailty. God invites all who are troubled to unite with his saving grace, where true rest awaits.

Pondering this verse provided me much-needed spiritual introspection. God's kind plan to minister to me has taught me to trust him more. I am leaning closer than ever to him, and my spirit is lighter. And I know, whatever the future holds, I want my journey to be colored deeper with his gentle companionship. Finally, I understand why I am here. And it feels great.

Thank you, Lord, for the ministry of your gentleness and for seeking me when I need rest.

Real wisdom, God's wisdom, begins with a holy life and is characterized by getting along with others. It is gentle and reasonable, overflowing with mercy and blessings, not hot one day and cold the next, not two-faced. You can develop a healthy, robust community that lives right with God and enjoy its results only if you do the hard work of getting along with each other, treating each other with dignity and honor.

JAMES 3:17–18 (MSG)

That's Bananas!

by Lisa-Anne Wooldridge

A gentle answer deflects anger, but harsh words make tempers flare.

PROVERBS 15:1 (NLT)

I'LL BE THE first to admit that I inherited some feisty genes and haven't always been good at keeping their natural expression in check. Worse than that, I think I'm funny and love to crack myself and others up. I was an impulsive, sarcastic, observant ten-year-old whose middle name should have been *Trouble*—because I could find it, start it, or land myself in it in two seconds flat!

As an adult, I still crack myself up, and my dearest friends think I'm hilarious. They have to; I put it in the contract. But I've learned to use my powers for good—most of the time—because the words I use create the world I live in. A very wise man once said something profound about the power of life and death being housed in the human mouth, and I can verify that claim. (Solomon. It was King Solomon. He was considered wise *despite* having a few too many wives!)

I've learned to use my humor gently, to build up instead of tear down. Where I used to launch Shakespeare-worthy insults to defend against injustice, now I look for words that will allow people to see themselves in light of their Maker, who calls them fearfully and wonderfully made.

The words I use create the world I live in.

Sometimes I still struggle with anger, frustration, and hostility. To be honest, the climate of our country doesn't help. The place this pops up the most is on social media. It's always a tug-of-war with words, whether I release them boldly or hold back with restraint. My intent is to reflect gentleness, goodness, and self-control. But often my passion for justice doesn't feel very gentle. Can you relate?

It can be difficult to see the imago Dei—the image of God—in people, especially on their worst days, but it's always there, waiting to be called to the surface. Have you ever seen someone yawn, say on a warm Sunday in July in a sleepy little church, and suddenly everyone is yawning? We're wired like that! All kinds of things are "contagious" within our species. So, if we act with gentleness, especially in response to harshness, we not only prevent ourselves from being infected with anger but also provide a layer of protection to people around us.

One afternoon, I had the opportunity to choose how I reacted when I came across a man absolutely losing his stuffing in a big box warehouse store. It was an already tense atmosphere, too crowded, with impatient people being inconsiderate and inconsiderate people being irate. To me, it felt like an icy storm cloud was gathering, and all hail was about to break loose!

The man rammed his cart into the cart of a woman parked by the produce displays as she picked through bananas. His face was red

A WORDGIRLS COLLECTIVE

as he yelled that she had blocked the aisle. I was regretting my shopping trip—an angry, potentially violent man within feet of me, no quick means of escape, and a terrified woman just trying to find some ripe bananas. She clearly did not want to engage in a rousing game of bumper carts! My inner ten-year-old immediately had something snarky to say. Instead, I turned my focus inward and asked the Lord to show me what I needed to see.

The items in his cart caught my eye as understanding flooded my mind. My ready sarcasm turned to gentle compassion.

"Sir, I can see you're trying to get home to take care of somebody sick." I gestured at the children's electrolyte drinks, the bag of rice, jars of applesauce, and a twin pack of sliced bread. That his frustration boiled over by the bananas clued me in that there was a sick child at home whose doctor had ordered the BRAT diet—bananas, rice, applesauce, and toast—to help keep food on the *inside* of the child and not all over their living room carpet. "Is there anything I can get for you? I know it's hot and crowded in here, but I'm happy to help you get what you need so you can get home faster."

He looked over at me, fully prepared to unleash his anger, when my words sank in, and the fury drained from his body.

Since he was still speechless, I added, "Here, take my wet wipes and trash bags. You probably need them more than I do."

He nodded.

I grabbed some bananas since I was closer and put them in the front of his cart. He looked shell-shocked, so I added, "Boy or girl? I'll pray for them to feel better."

His eyes lit up, and he finally found his voice. "How? Why? Who? What?"

I stopped him before he could get to "where" and just said, "God knows. You're just trying to be a good dad, and your kid probably has something awful coming out of both ends, right? It's probably like a

GATHER THE GOODNESS

horror film at your house right now and you're stuck in this zoo with the pokiest people on the planet." I smiled at him, hoping I was giving off compassion and comfort and not "crazy."

He pushed his cart toward me and said, "Thank you. I'm sorry I yelled. It's my son. My wife is sick too. She usually does all the shopping, but they both have fevers and some kind of stomach flu. Maybe you should just pray for all of us because I'm not feeling so good myself."

I said I'd be happy to do that as he pushed his cart toward the front. I stopped long enough to send up a missile of gratitude and prayers for the man and his family before I headed back to get more trash bags and baby wipes. And hand sanitizer—the biggest size they had. The feeling of tension had gone out of the store, and I noticed people were being thoughtful and considerate with each other.

As I walked, I could hear a litany of polite words. "Excuse me, may I just grab one of those?" and "Let me get that down for you," followed by "Thank you so much," and "My pleasure!" It was as if I'd been transported to Miss Emily's Finishing School for Suburbanites!

I thoroughly enjoyed watching people truly see one another and treat each other with gentleness and respect. I got my groceries and hauled myself out of there before someone curtsied and asked me to the cotillion.

> *Father of all kinds of funny people, help me see the people around me in the light of your love and open my eyes to all the ways they are made in your image. Help me hold up a mirror that reflects your love and grace so they see themselves in you too. Help me grow in gentleness as I use my words to change my world. And give me a soft heart full of soft answers for those who need them.*

In Gentleness He Stooped

by Joanie Shawhan

The little girl huddled, hiding in a dark corner,
Ashamed of her stained dress and tangled hair.
She clutched a tattered doll, its arm
    torn from the socket.
A button eye dangled from a few slim threads.

A light shone. She squinted, shielding her eyes,
Peeked one open, dazzled by its beam.
A white-robed man with long hair and beard
Drew close, emanating the light.

Trembling, she clasped her doll tighter,
Drawn to his smile. But why was he here?
He held out his arms, requesting her doll,
All that she had—her treasured possession.

With her doll in his hands, what would he do?
Laugh—tear her apart—throw her away?
Faced with persistence, her little hands quivered,
She kissed the doll goodbye and handed her away.

But instead of derision, he cradled her treasure,
Pressed close to his heart, cherished and precious.
He stretched forth his hand, beckoned the girl come,
Eyes fixed on her, full of love and compassion.

Forward she inched, not sure what to expect.
He drew her close, a tender embrace,
In the arms of her Savior, secure and protected,
Cleansed, clothed in white—his unmerited favor.

The doll, a persona of her old human nature,
Once entangled in sin, now spiritually reborn.
In gentleness, he stooped with his
    wraparound presence.
The lost child he rescued—now filled with his essence.

The Enemy of Gentleness

by Denise Margaret Ackerman

Always be humble and gentle. Be patient with each other.

EPHESIANS 4:2 (NLT)

THERE WERE PEOPLE everywhere! We shuffled through the port's crowded checkpoints, dragging four bulky suitcases, anxious to finally get settled on our stately vessel. Once aboard, we faced hordes of impatient passengers gathered in front of the overwhelmed elevators. Jim and I decided to climb seven flights of stairs to our stateroom. The room was inviting, but we were too hungry to stay put. We returned to the staircase and scaled two floors for the dining area.

Long lines jammed the buffet. Once we finally selected our food, there was no place to sit!

We had booked this eighteen-day trip to combat the winter blues. We felt confident the extended break from the brutal New York winter weather would refresh our spirits and give us a renewed perspective.

GATHER THE GOODNESS

After several days of being surrounded by people, I began to wrestle with impatience and frustration, both displeasing to the Lord. It wasn't long before I realized that I would not enjoy this vacation if I continued to allow the multitudes of fellow travelers to bother me.

Retreating to the solitude of our cabin, I searched God's Word for guidance in changing my attitude. Paul, the writer of the book of Philippians, describes the attributes of a gentle spirit and directs believers to let those qualities be known to others.[78] Graciousness, unselfishness, mercy, tolerance, and patience were all traits I struggled with. Although I didn't express my angst outwardly, I'm sure my face and body language showed frustration as I moved in and around my fellow shipmates.

I asked the Lord to show me why I reacted so negatively to pushy people. He revealed the answer to my question in chapter five of Galatians.[79] *It is your sinful nature, Denise.*

Selfishness is the enemy of a gentle spirit.

Instead of being gentle and caring toward others, I acted selfishly. I began to think about Jesus and his response to the thousands of people who flocked to him. He looked at them with compassion. My focus when responding to crowds of people was nothing like the Lord's. My vacation had become about me. The fact that others were constantly in *my* way, bumping into *me*, and stepping ahead of *me* had ruffled *my* feathers. When is it okay for believers to completely focus on themselves rather than share love and concern for those around them?

---

78. Philippians 4:4–5 (AMP)
79. Galatians 5:17 (AMP)

To further solidify my need for an attitude adjustment, the Lord also gently reminded me that I had prayed for opportunities to share my love for him with others before we left on our adventure. I repented for my lack of compassion and prayed he would help me to stop being bothered by the many people in my way.

My time spent praying and reading God's Word taught me an important lesson. When I'm feeling grumpy toward others, I need to ask the Lord to show me why. I've learned that selfishness is the enemy of a gentle spirit. That afternoon, I left our peaceful cabin with a different perspective—my fellow travelers needed the Lord! I purposed to gently demonstrate his loving-kindness to those waiting at elevators, standing in buffet lines, and searching for a lunch table.

Dear heavenly Father, thank you for teaching me through your Word and prayer. I want my life to honor you, to gently display your compassion for each person. Please keep my heart sensitive to those around me. Help me to show your love in all I do.

Wardrobe Malfunctions

by Kathy Carlton Willis

Since God chose you to be the holy people he loves, you must clothe yourselves with tenderhearted mercy, kindness, humility, gentleness, and patience.

COLOSSIANS 3:12 (NLT)

OVER THE YEARS, I've had many clothing mishaps. Wardrobe malfunctions. Part of the problem is that I'm not a fancy girl. Basic comfort defines what I reach for in the closet most days. The other issue is that I'm never sure what space my belly will take up in a garment.

I'm glad I can have better results when I clothe myself in the attitudes and actions of God. Let's look at these garments.

- **Tenderhearted mercy:** compassion, a deep empathy and concern for others' suffering
- **Kindness:** intentional acts of goodness and generosity

- **Humility:** recognizing my weaknesses and not seeking self-glory

- **Gentleness:** quiet strength, a soft demeanor, avoiding harshness

- **Patience:** discipline to endure hardship and wait without resentment

Whenever I see the phrase "put on" or "clothe yourself" in Scripture, I realize I can't just acquire those things passively, but I have to be intentional about actively putting on these garments. I tend to pick up traits from others when I'm around them a lot. If they have a different accent, my talking might sound similar to the way they speak. If they are funny, I find myself getting funnier. If they are serious, I am low-key. Similarly, when I stay in God's presence, I can become like him.

I can have better results when I clothe myself in the attitudes and actions of God.

This kind of "putting on" isn't behavior modification or self-improvement. It's a transformation from the inside out. The attitudes change before the actions do. It's not about legalistically following a set of rules but becoming more like God. We start by putting on the mind of Christ. "Have this same attitude in yourselves which was in Christ Jesus [look to Him as your example in selfless humility]."[80]

Because the Holy Spirit is active in me, when I'm aware of his presence, he stimulates empathy in me for others. That empathy, along with discernment, helps me put on all these garments. When I can

---

80. Philippians 2:5 (AMP)

empathize with someone and sense what they are going through and feeling, I care enough to be compassionate. And because of that, intentional acts of kindness come to mind. I realize they are wounded, and a gesture of gentleness will be more welcome than coming in like a whirlwind to rescue them. And I'll need a dose of patience to wait for the results—or to keep showing kindness, even when the other party doesn't respond the way I hope. They will not always appreciate what I've done for them. I also need to examine my motive. Not to fix them but to serve them because I care.

They are wounded, and a gesture of gentleness will be more welcome than coming in like a whirlwind to rescue them.

The next verse after our focus passage says, "And regardless of what else you put on, wear love. It's your basic, all-purpose garment. Never be without it."[81] It looks like my desire for a basic garment isn't a bad thing. And I realize, just like these other virtues, they aren't meant to work solely on the inside of us. I don't even think you can keep love inside. It always expresses itself outwardly. But we first have to believe it and receive it inwardly. Just like Colossians 3:12 says: to realize we are God's beloved. God chose us. Despite all our wardrobe malfunctions, he loves humankind. And knowing that helps us truly be kind.

It's important to note that Paul is careful not to emphasize what we can do in the way of good works to earn the favor of the Father. No, he shows us the good works that flow from God and encourages us to be all in regarding receiving and giving love so that we become like him. Growth doesn't happen alone. And growth isn't merely for our benefit but for the benefit of God's kingdom.

---

81. Colossians 3:14 (MSG)

GATHER THE GOODNESS

Often, our tendency in our humanness is the opposite of the virtues in Colossians. Instead of tenderhearted mercy, we want revenge. Rather than kindness, selfishness. Instead of humility, ego. Not gentleness but harshness. Patience isn't natural, but irritation, intolerance, and impulsiveness are.

Let's see what we can do to become more like God. Tenderhearted mercy, kindness, humility, gentleness, and patience. Keep these virtues in mind as you process the steps and questions below.

Strip Off the Old Garments[82]

1. Recognize the sinful acts and desires that aren't like God.

2. Put these things to death because they separate you from God.

3. When the desire to sin resurfaces, go through the process of getting rid of it. Strip it off and get it out of your closet. When you don't have access to it, it's harder to put it back on!

How to Dress for Godly Success[83]

1. Put on the shaper garment of peace so that it smooths out all the bumps and makes your outfit look more attractive on you. When it is becoming on you, what are you becoming?

2. Be thankful. How do you cultivate gratitude? By doing it over and over again. It doesn't always come naturally.

---

82. Colossians 3:5–9
83. Colossians 3:15–17

3. Live in God's Word and let it live in you. This is where we gain wisdom.
4. Don't just keep what you know of God to yourself. As you grow, help others grow.
5. Let the good God stuff in you overflow from you. Keep on singing. Sing the song God has planted in you. When you are thankful, you can't help but sing!
6. Whatever you are doing, do it because of Jesus. Your actions are the way you thank him. This is where the virtues mentioned in Colossians 3:12 show up.

Preventing Wardrobe Malfunctions

Ask yourself,

- In what areas do I need to cultivate more godliness?
- How do these "garments" make a difference in my relationships? If I have a relationship that is struggling right now, which one of these attributes do I choose to incorporate more to see if it can turn the dysfunction to function? Change the funk to fun?
- Who in my life tends to push my buttons? Which one of these virtues would help me respond in a healthier way to their hurtful words and actions?

Oh, Father, I'm not good at this. As much as I struggle to dress well on the outside, I also struggle to clothe myself with your virtues and attributes. I'm sure glad I don't have to be good at it. I simply need to stay aware of your presence in me and at work to help me express your love to others.

But in your hearts honor Christ the Lord as holy, always being prepared to make a defense to anyone who asks you for a reason for the hope that is in you; yet do it with gentleness and respect.

1 PETER 3:15 (ESV)

Takes a Big Dog to Weigh a Ton

by Beth Kirkpatrick

Let your speech always be with grace, seasoned with salt, that you may know how you ought to answer each one.

Colossians 4:6 (nkjv)

"WELL, IT TAKES a big dog to weigh a ton." Conversations with my German grandpa always delighted me. His impish sense of humor, coupled with his insatiable curiosity, made for entertaining interactions sprinkled with old jokes and adages. Someone who was a little kooky "didn't have all her cups in the cupboard." And I lost count of how many times the dogfish chased the catfish up a tree and was saved by the sawfish. We had to be prepared for some silliness if we asked Grandpa what was new.

Grandpa lived with us in California during the cool fall and winter months and returned to his native Wisconsin for the spring and summer. Though afflicted with painful arthritis, he never complained, just bounced up and down to "limber up," and he sometimes needed a little extra help to get his "hind leg" into the car. He loved game shows and expressed deep disappointment when the contestants didn't listen to him about the prices they guessed. He once reported that a couple had won a trip to Venus! (We finally figured out it was Venice.)

Everyone knew Grandpa loved to fish. As a special treat, his friends took him out on the ocean, leaving early in the morning. On those days, Grandpa explained, "I get all ready the night before, sleep in my recliner, and when they knock on my door, I 'rare' up, and I'm ready to go!"

Young and old loved to visit with Grandpa. His lifetime of experiences provided a wealth of stories and observations about the world around him. He enjoyed helping out by sharpening knives, shelling walnuts from our trees, and he ate all the burned cookies because he said charcoal was good for your teeth. (He had dentures.)

Every day, I watched my grandpa spend time reading his Bible and prayer book. He read aloud but under his breath—reading glasses perched on his nose, hands folded, and speckled bald head bowed reverently.

Let us seek out and appreciate models of God's gentle grace.

Grandpa didn't present himself as a know-it-all or take center stage with his opinions. His gentleness showed up in conversations. He stood ready to hear your story, to share something funny, to invite you into his next scheme or adventure. (Did I tell you about the time he pinned down a rattlesnake by the head with the tip of his fishing pole and got my little cousins to come kill it with rocks?)

It was a true blessing to be his granddaughter, and he taught me so much about honoring God, enjoying life, and loving others. He could and would talk to anyone, and they'd both end up smiling or chuckling. I am so thankful for his example of grace-filled, humor-salted conversation. And he was right—it takes a big dog to weigh a ton!

Thank you, Lord, for my earthly models of your grace. Help me to seek them out and appreciate them. Teach me to fill my conversations with gentleness, seasoned with humor and understanding.

Our Contributors

A WORDGIRLS COLLECTIVE

DENISE MARGARET ACKERMAN shares life lessons from her spiritual journey as she seeks to encourage readers in their own walk with the Lord. Denise is a contributing author for *Guideposts* and has published devotionals in five WordGirls books. Married for over fifty years to her high school sweetheart, she and her husband, Jim, play pickleball to stay fit for their eight active grandchildren. Reach Denise at dackerman.0922@gmail.com or on Facebook.

MINDY CANTRELL's life passion is forwarding the same love and emotional healing God poured out on her to all those around her. She lives with husband and cat-child, Ramjet, in the Texas "boonies." Mindy spends her time ministering to ladies' groups, and visiting daughter, granddaughter, and veteran son-in-law in North Carolina. Her devotionals can be found in other WordGirls collectives. Catch up with Mindy and read her grief blog at mindycantrell.com.

SALLY FERGUSON enjoys connecting with women and helping them find encouragement from God's Word. She is a retreat junkie and created a resource for planners. Sally lives in Western New York with her husband and is working on a Bible study for caregivers. Check out the book giveaways at sallyferguson.net and the retreat planner at bit.ly/PlanRtWkbk.

GATHER THE GOODNESS

CAROLYN GASTON, a retired teacher and administrator, now spends her time threading words together and crafting rag rugs. She brings hope to her readers and helps them weave their unique stories together for God's glory. She is a part-time ESL instructor and leads two ladies' Bible studies—one in English and one in Spanish. Carolyn loves spending time with her family, camping, and baking for her ten grandchildren.

BECKI JAMES is an ally to all who desire to live in the presence of God. With an "old friend" flair, she gently guides hearts to the throne of God. Whether she's ministering with microphone or pen, Becki's way with words catches the spirits of all ages with fresh direction. She enjoys resting by the water, gathering at a table of friends, and loving on family. Find her at beckijames.com.

BETH KIRKPATRICK is a wife, mom, and grandmother who enjoys reading books and laughing with her friends. She strives to be a light for Jesus by being a good listener and sharing encouragement with others. She has contributed to several WordGirls collectives. After many years of working with elementary students, Beth now works with adults in a literacy ministry, Learning Matters! You can contact her at bethakirk@yahoo.com.

A WORDGIRLS COLLECTIVE

SANDY LIPSKY's purpose in writing about real-life encounters is to be a blessing. During the day she writes, teaches piano, and cares for her household. Nighttime finds her reading. Sandy has been a WordGirl since 2018 and is a contributing author to five previous WordGirl's collective books. Her latest work appears in a compilation entitled *Whiskers, Wags, and Woofs*. She enjoys Georgia's seasons and spending time with her husband, daughter, and playful pups. sandylipsky.com

KOLLEEN LUCARIELLO is a passionate speaker, author, and advocate for women seeking growth in their faith. She has a heart for empowering others. Kolleen shares biblical insights with authenticity, encouraging women to embrace their God-given identity and purpose. She is the author of *#beYOU: Change Your Identity One Letter at a Time* and the co-executive director of the women's ministry, Activ8Her, Inc. Her warmth and wisdom make her a trusted voice in women's ministry.

CHARLAINE MARTIN loves helping women discover how life is always an adventure with God. You can find her tending her garden, cycling local bike trails with her Boaz, and putzing the skies in their single-engine plane together. She also loves sharing tickle bugs with their grandchildren. Charlaine is an author in several WordGirls compilations, as well as *Renewed Christmas Blessings*, and writes devotions for Crossmap.com. She is also a speaker and Bible teacher. charlainemartin.com

GATHER THE GOODNESS

DIANA LEAGH MATTHEWS shares God's love through her story from rebel to redeemed. Her day job is as a volunteer coordinator, but at night she writes and hunts genealogy. She gives programs as a speaker, teacher, and vocalist, and presents historical monologues. Leagh (pronounced Lee) is the author of *Carol of the Rooms, Forever Changed, 90 Breath Prayers for the Caregiver*, and others in the Breath Prayers series. Connect with her at DianaLeaghMatthews.com.

JANICE METOT thrives on comforting others with the same comfort God has given her. She found her voice as a writer, nurturing other women like herself. Janice serves in worship ministry and uses a lifetime of experience teaching and encouraging others in their faith. Her words offer perspective and hope to all she meets, inviting you to pause, have a cup of coffee, and reflect for a while.

Sharing the gospel through writing and speaking is one of **BETTY PREDMORE**'s favorite things to do. She engages audiences with her easy, conversational style. Her words make women pause and ponder the possibilities of a beautiful life with Christ. As an author, Christian communicator, and ministry leader, Betty uses every opportunity to encourage women to live their best life in Christ and overcome the strongholds that hold them captive. momsenseinc.org

A WORDGIRLS COLLECTIVE

PATTIE REITZ is a proud military chaplain's wife and mother of two daughters. She loves reading, writing, and coffee. With each military move, God provides her with fun adventures in teaching English. Her writing is included in the devotional *Praying Through Loneliness* and the WordGirls books *Sage, Salt & Sunshine* and *Love, Joy & Peace*. She and her husband make their home wherever God and the Air Force send them.

VICTORIA HANAN ROMO is an award-winning writer, entrepreneur, and author of *The Ballad of Cinderella Jones* and *Life with Levi*. With wry observations, a penchant for comedy, and life experiences ranging from unearthing Peruvian mummies to living at the YWCA, her work rarely leaves readers bored. Victoria and her family live in Castroville, Texas, a picturesque river town full of cool old homes and quirky denizens—including her magnificent trio.

JOANIE SHAWHAN shares true-life stories, offering her reader an eyewitness view of the action. Her Selah Awards finalist book, *In Her Shoes: Dancing in the Shadow of Cancer*, reflects the value of "your story plus my story become our stories." An ovarian cancer survivor and registered nurse, Joanie speaks to medical students in the Survivors Teaching Students program. She co-founded an ovarian cancer social group: The Fried Eggs—Sunny-Side Up. Visit Joanie at joanieshawhan.com.

GATHER THE GOODNESS

ROBIN STEINWEG finds life "Sweet in the Middle"—like the creamy center of a sandwich cookie! She writes, ghostwrites, and edits. Her writing can be found in each of the WordGirls collective books, and in such publications as *Keys for Kids*, *The Upper Room*, and *Today's Christian Woman*. Read Robin's daily prayers for parents/grandparents at Prayerenting on Facebook, and bits of positivity with songs on her YouTube channel, both found at robinsteinweg.com.

BARB SYVERTSON enjoys writing things down. And then she likes turning those scraps into a readable piece that shows others the love of God in her life. She and her husband have three married sons and eight delightful grandkids. When she's not writing things down, she loves to go to libraries, thrift shops, fabric stores, and on hikes. Spending time with family is her favorite pastime. She welcomes your feedback at barbsyvertson@gmail.com.

JULIA THOMPSON lives with her husband near Jamestown, New York. They raised three adopted children with special needs. A Bible study teacher, Julie uses her writing as another outlet for sharing God's goodness and love. Poetry, short stories, and devotions bring her joy. She is working on a novel about three generations of women who search for purpose and legacy. Julia is a member of WordGirls and can be reached at julialaura125@gmail.com.

A WORDGIRLS COLLECTIVE

JONI TOPPER is a compelling storyteller who longs to look like Jesus. As a pastor's wife, mom, grandmother, author, worship leader, and speaker, she wants to exhibit God's glory. Joni is passionate about "being" the church. Her debut book, *The Power of a Well-Placed Yes: God's Abundant Faithfulness in a Small Church* launched in March 2024. She has also contributed to five other books and numerous publications. See more at morninggloryministry.com.

HALLY J. WELLS is a retired school counselor and recent empty nester who writes about faith, parenting, and mental illness. Beautifully awed and exhausted by her students and her own sampler pack of biological, adopted, step, and foster kids, Hally helps overwhelmed parents find practical answers, impactful resources, faith-family support, and divine wisdom—"digging deep enough to find the good stuff, reaching high enough to find the best!" Visit Hally at hallyjwells.com.

KATHY CARLTON WILLIS, known as God's Grin Gal, writes and speaks with a balance of funny and faith, whimsy and wisdom. Kathy is passionate about helping believers love God and his Word despite the trials of life. Her messages inspire grin-worthy moments despite groan-worthy experiences. Grin and grow along with her as she shares her boldly practical tips, tools, and takeaways. Explore Kathy's Grin Gal line of books at kathycarltonwillis.com.

GATHER THE GOODNESS

DAWN MARIE WILSON, an author and Bible teacher, has served God for fifty-plus years in revival ministry and missions. She fleshes out scriptural truths through her writing at Crosswalk.com and her blog, TruthTalkWithDawn.com. Her mission is "encouraging wise, biblical choices through God's truth talk." Dawn coauthored *Truth Talk for Hurting Hearts: Discover Peace & Comfort Through God's Perspective*. She and her husband live in Southern California.

LISA-ANNE WOOLDRIDGE is inspired by illuminated manuscripts and stained-glass windows. Her heartwarming true stories have been published in several popular collections. Her second novel in The Cozy Cat Bookstore Mysteries, *The Rose and Crown*, is now available online. She lives in the land of mountains and valleys that drink in the rain of heaven—otherwise known as Oregon, or you may find her at Lisa-Anne.net.

Acknowledgments

This book was made possible due to some very special people. Named below are those who believed in the gift God placed inside of us. Thank you for gathering the goodness and pouring it into our lives. We want to acknowledge your support and help.

We have grateful gratitudes for:

Our buddy editors. Each writing project in our book was edited by at least one buddy editor before the contributing author submitted the piece. Some had input from multiple buddies. We couldn't have done this project without you. Your gentle correction made a difference. In addition to the contributing authors helping one other (a beautiful thing to watch!), we benefited from feedback from Jessica Birdwell, Darlene Hart, Lori Lipsky, and Alicia Willsie. Thank you for helping us out.

Our WordMama, Kathy Carlton Willis. You gathered a wonderful array of writers around God's bountiful table. You invited us to share the goodness of God stored up in our hearts, revealing the treasures and stories we have hidden there. You set a beautiful table and encouraged us to bring our best offerings. You helped us keep in mind our guests, readers who are hungry to taste and see that the Lord is good. You created an environment so we feel like we're coming home when we collaborate words. You propelled us to excellence in a grace space where we learn what the industry expects. Not only do you see value in our stories but in us—and you helped us see it too.

Our families and friends. You cheered us on and managed without us so we could write. How kind of you to support our dreams and cherish our words. You faithfully showed us your love and approval, which helped us overcome big-time imposter syndrome thoughts and feelings. Every time you read and review our work, you help us succeed. *Gather the Goodness* is possible in part because of you. Thank you for affirming the gifts in us and encouraging us to use them as we write.

Our editor and book designer, Michelle Rayburn. You gathered all of our words and wrapped them into a beautiful gift. The wrapped box (the book) edited to industry standards and also to match the intent of God's Word as well as our written words. The ribbon and bow of our beautiful gift is the artistic book cover design and the creative interior design. Thank you for caring enough to make *Gather the Goodness* everything it can be and not settling for anything less. We are proud to have another professional book in our collective.

Our churches. We value the fellowship of faith. Because of our heavenly Father, we are family.

Our Lord. May this book bring you all the glory. It is because of you and your Word that we have words. Your Spirit is the source of kindness, goodness, faithfulness, and gentleness. We're dedicating this book to you and ask that you flow through each reader as they abide in you. What a privilege to be your WordGirls.

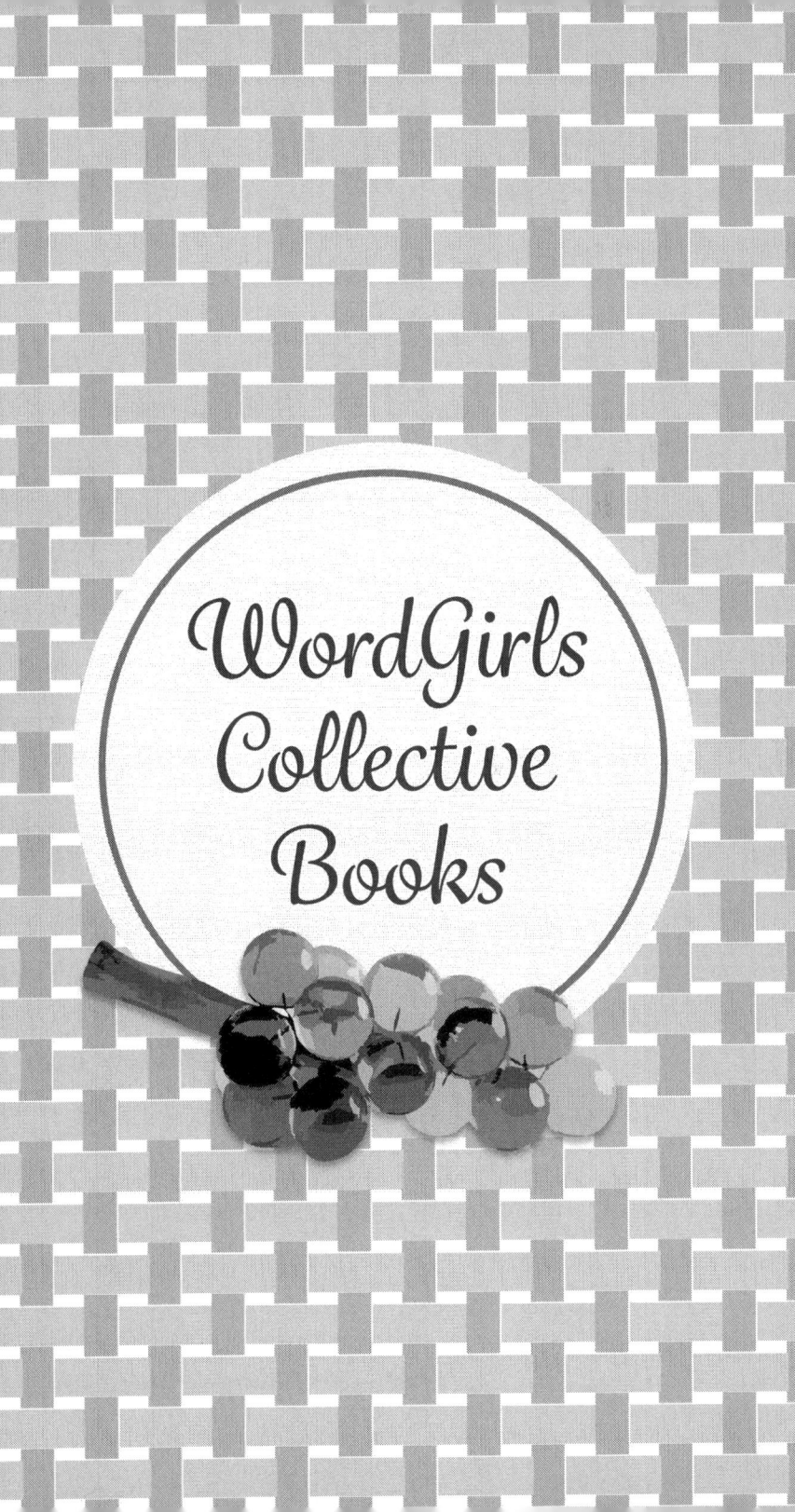

WordGirls Collective Books

GATHER THE GOODNESS

WordGirls Collective Books

OUR ESSAY COLLECTIVES

Live & Learn

When we say, "Well, live and learn!" we think of surprising outcomes.

You'll relate to these essays if you're tired of figuring out God's guidance the hard way. *Live & Learn* features first-person stories about unexpected lessons from twenty-seven WordGirls. God uses big and small circumstances for monumental life-transforming moments. Even the insignificant can make a big impact when we pay attention.

The expression "live and learn" has been passed down through time to mean we often grasp life best by experience. Some of us catch on the hard way or take multiple times to comprehend and apply this sort of training.

Come discover the unexpected with us as you read along about:

- Childhood life schooling
- Hilarious ahas! with ha-has
- Embarrassment as a teacher
- Turning points in life
- Stranger-than-life teachers
- Tough-but-tender love

You will find these essays to be a balance of funny and serious, dialogue and narration, weighty and light.

Our prayer is that *Live & Learn* will help you have your own studies in God's classroom. Be on the lookout. It just might happen when you least expect it!

A WORDGIRLS COLLECTIVE

Sage, Salt & Sunshine

Introducing forty-eight life shapers and difference makers, and the traits that make them extraordinary women.

Sage, Salt & Sunshine features first-person stories about women who made a difference in this world. Allow the storytelling narratives and scenes to sweep you up into the lives of these exceptional women. Together we can figure out this life thing much better than trying to go it alone.

Who are our spiritual mothers? They are the ones who spent time with us when it wasn't convenient. Their lives patterned the life of Christ to us in a way we could emulate and pass on to the next generation. They didn't get everything right, but they showed love when we needed it most. They helped us fall in love with Jesus and made the Bible come alive to us. They not only helped us to grow spiritually, but they showed us practical, everyday ways of living life.

Our prayer is that *Sage, Salt & Sunshine* will motivate you to show gratitude to your spiritual mother and inspire you to be a life-changing influence on other women watching you.

GATHER THE GOODNESS

OUR DEVOTIONALS

Love, Joy & Peace

Together on the road trip of life.

Pack your bags and join the WordGirls for a road trip with God. In *Love, Joy & Peace*, twenty-eight writers come together to explore the profound truths about love, joy, and peace that echo throughout Scripture.

With eighty-nine thought-provoking devotions, this collective provides a roadmap for navigating life's twists and turns with grace and faith. Through real-life stories paired with poignant Bible verses and heartfelt prayers, you'll find road signs that celebrate God's abundant blessings everywhere.

From the exhilarating highs to the peaceful valleys, join us as we embrace the "van life," infused with the love, joy, and peace that only God can provide. And let's have a little fun along the way—no hippie head trips needed for those psychedelic colors. Sure, wear your bell-bottom pants! Open up your mind and heart to see what God says, and you'll be well on your way.

We pray these words will lead you on your own road trip toward love, joy, and peace.

Snapshots of Hope & Heart

When we hear the word snapshots . . . we think moments.

In this WordGirls collective, we researched what God's Word says about the topics of hope and heart. *Snapshots of Hope & Heart* includes eighty-four devotions written by thirty-four WordGirls. The authors inserted stories, much like snapshots, to help us capture a true-to-life inspirational insight fitting for the daily Scripture. We hope the takeaways will stick with you throughout the day, similar to the memory of a snapshot long after you've tucked it away.

Enjoy taking a moment with God as you read this devotional. Take your own snapshots as you look through our album of hope and heart.

A WORDGIRLS COLLECTIVE

Our prayer is that these words will deliver word pictures of hope and heart to save to your mind's photo album. In that frame of reference, the Bible is the faith family album deserving to be passed down through the generations.

Wit, Whimsy & Wisdom

Seeking special time with God each day?

Wit, Whimsy & Wisdom is here to be your guide. In each devotion, look for a concept you can refer back to in your thoughts as you go about your day. The stories will give you some grins, some grace, and some grit to help you through the struggles you face, as well as help you celebrate moments of victory.

This three-month devotional is divided into five relevant sections. Feel free to read it straight through or choose what you need that day. Our sections feature Worship & Prayer, Humor, Family, Spiritual Growth, and Women's Issues.

Wit, Whimsy & Wisdom was the first WordGirls devotional, designed to use God's Word and the words of WordGirls to help you fall in love even more with the Word made flesh—Jesus.

Our desire is for you to find nuggets within these pages that make you think, inspire you to worship, and even give you a few laughs along the way.

Made in the USA
Columbia, SC
25 May 2025